Divine
Ye

TONY MYERS

Copyright © 2018 Tony Myers

All rights reserved.
ISBN 13: 9781728924687

All rights reserved. This book or any portion thereof may not be reproduced or used in any manner whatsoever without the express written permission of the publisher except for the use of brief quotations in a book review.

EDITED BY: Tess Sainz
CO-EDITED BY: Diana Jamerson
COVER DESIGN BY: AKIRA GRAPHICZ

All scripture quotations are from the King James Version of the Bible unless otherwise noted.
The Bible, King James Version. 1987 printing, Public Domain.

Scripture quotations marked (NLT) are taken from:
The Holy Bible, New Living Translation. Copyright© 1996, 2004, 2007 by Tyndale House Foundation. Used by permission of Tyndale House Publishers, Inc, Carol
Stream, Illinois 60188. All rights reserved

DEDICATION

This book is dedicated to Christ Jesus. May those who read it, have a true experience of His love for us. My wife Deb, without whom I may not have survived long enough to write this book. My readers: may your search for healing end as you open these pages and can truly acknowledge your healing.

Table of Contents

DEDICATION..iii

Table of Contents..iv

ACKNOWLEDGMENTS..vi

REVIEWS..vii

FOREWORD...ix

PREFACE..xii

1 MINDING THE FLESH..1

2 DAYS OF OLD..8

3 GODS SPIRIT IN MAN..16

4 OLD WAYS GONE...25

5 PLUGGED INTO THE SOURCE......................................32

6 THE FIRST BORN...39

7 NO LONGER MERE MORTALS......................................48

8 MERCY AND RIGHTEOUSNESS....................................55

9 RECOGNIZING, NOT RECEIVING..................................62

10 A LIE IS LIE..72

11 IT DOES APPLY TO YOU...77

12 MYSTERY REVEALED..83

13 ANGEL ARMIES..90

14 DEFEATED DEMONS...97

15 TRASH TRADITIONS	105
16 FOOD OR HOLY SPIRIT	114
17 HOLY INTIMACY	123
18 WRAPPING IT UP	128
ABOUT THE AUTHOR	130
MORE FROM TONY	131

ACKNOWLEDGMENTS

My dearest wife for putting up with me.
Diana Jamerson, always available for a witty comment.
Oleg Aristo, who I leaned on for his opinion and wisdom.
Tess Sainz, she is a true encourager.
My readers, your feedback is always appreciated.

REVIEWS

Tony Myers is my personal friend and like a modern-day Apostle Paul. I never knew Tony when he was an atheist Christian abuser, but I'm proud to know him now! His wonderful encounter with the Living Jesus, his subsequent physical healing from "incurable" and "untreatable" illness and his release from a "certain death" is nothing short of amazing!
Was this Gift or his ability to BE well already on the inside of Tony? Did Tony already possess something (or Someone) that perhaps he was not fully aware of at the time of illness? Did Jesus, 2000 years ago, purchase MORE than our spiritual salvation?In these pages, Tony addresses the Divine Nature that now resides in every one of us, the power that God's indwelling Holy Spirit presence provides and makes available for all, and our use of this amazing Gift.This beautiful, timely message is consistent with what Jesus revealed to and modeled for His earthly followers. It's consistent with the events and words recorded in Holy Scripture.No hocus pocus, and no religious rhetoric here.... just pure and simple gospel Truth expressed through a regular guy.BE still and know....BE healed!!~Peg Spicknall, Atlanta, GA

This book will teach you how to use the power we have as believers to command our own healing… and helps you to understand how the author came to the revelation and understanding he writes and teachers about in this book. The amazing examples and personal stories given are very encouraging and easy to understand. I respect the fact that the author of this book has lived this out personally and has found success and healing through the revelation given to him. I hope that every person who reads this book will be as motivated, challenged, and inspired as I was to start walking in the supernatural. ~Natalie Dicks, Zimbabwe

I am so excited about Tony's new book and highly recommend everyone to read it. How many times have you read a book about healing and found so much confusion. This book is written with different words so there is no confusion and so much more to phrases used in church paraphrases. ~Joyce Jacobs, Salisbury, MO

This book is a necessity for anyone looking for the manifestation of a healing and is a perfect closure to Tony's first two books. Tony Myers digs deep and makes it almost impossible to not see your healing! ~Doni Jo Vaughn, East Jordan, MI

This book is amazing! As a person who is in need of healing, I have studied healing a lot & some of the things I was reading and hearing did not really make sense to me… How do people get healed when someone prays for them if they have to do all the things people say? It would discourage me because I would get prayed for, I would even travel hours to get prayed for, & it didn't work. In this book, Tony cuts through to the core of healing. He shows you the simplicity of it and how attainable it is when so many times, we… feel like it is out of reach because we have too much sin, are not quoting enough scripture, etc. …it answered many questions for me… Thank you, Tony, for a great book!!!!! ~Carla Cave Williams, Traskwood, AR

FOREWORD

When I first heard about Tony Myers and his story of near-instant healing of paralysis, my heart was moved by his testimony in a unique way. It's not very often at all that healings from extreme medical conditions happen, even in the spirit-filled circles. It's even much less common to hear of someone receiving that type of healing on their own, without a prayer minister. After I had read Tony's book, "The Lord Jesus Healed Me," which detailed the brutal reality of a man living with a debilitating condition for years, one thing really stood out for me. That one thing was how quickly he was able to receive his healing directly from Jesus Christ, on his own, especially if you consider it against the backdrop of the severity of his medical condition.

I have been a purposeful student of divine healing for the past several years. Over those years, I have seen and read hundreds if not thousands of testimonies of people healed of various diseases. That exposure, combined with my own experience praying for hundreds of people with various health issues, taught me several things. One of the most important lessons which I have learned about God and his kingdom was this: what God does for one, he is willing and able to do for all. This truth nugget is simple yet quite profound. It will unlock the power of anyone else's testimony to work in your own life. And that's exactly why the author's testimony got me excited about the new level of possibilities with God.

When Tony was healed of that severe, life-threatening medical condition, he spent a year and a half going through the Scriptures to see what exactly caused his healing to take place in such a short order. Very importantly, he didn't take a magical and irrational path of ascribing his healing to an unrepeatable "sovereign act of God." Instead, his mindset was more like this: if it worked for one - it must work for all. Fortunately, the author was a relatively new believer at the time and his mind wasn't pre-programmed by years of religious conditioning.

I am very glad that Tony decided to travel the path of seeking further revelation about the cornerstone principles which undergird divine health and healing. Bodily healing was part and parcel of the ministry of Jesus Christ, and it's still a vital and indispensable part of the Gospel today. The book that you are holding in your hands is the result of the years-long process of the author tapping into God's truths about divine healing and of him test-driving those truths in real life situations.

The most important aspects of effective faith for healing have to do with our thoughts, beliefs, and expectations. Most of these exist on a sub-conscious level. You can't see those sorts of things with your eyes. In my opinion, that's one of the areas that this book excels at. It shows you how you can identify and eliminate several limiting beliefs when it comes to getting healing for yourself. In a way, it can be said that this book picks up where so many other teachings trail off.

There are very few resources in today's Christian marketplace which would teach you a practical, applicable process of how you can walk in your own divine healing and health. There are books out there which teach you that divine healing is for you today. But believing that you have a right to something is not the same as knowing how to make use of those rights. Then there are books on how to minister healing to the sick. Those are great but believing God for your own healing presents a unique set of challenges which is not present when you pray for others. Not the least of those challenges is dealing with the story that your symptoms and your pain are trying to tell you. This book spends a good deal of space dealing specifically with these sorts of questions.

The benefits of this book are several. For one, it shows that the process of walking in divine healing is fundamentally simple. It may not always be easy, but it certainly is simple. The book does a great job taking the reader down to the nitty-gritty of what makes divine healing work. Please don't be fooled by the book's down-to-earth, conversational style. You may think that it can't possibly be that simple. Thinking that it has to be more complicated is, in fact, one of the fleshly mindsets which make it more difficult to walk in divine healing.

The problem is not that the truth is too simple. The problem is that we have too many competing ideas which redirect our beliefs from the truth and thereby render the truth powerless. In typical scenarios, our religious traditions, superstitious self-talk, and materialistic narratives consume a lot of our focus, so the divine truths barely receive any of our focus and very little of our attention. All those other things siphon off our precious heart resources.

That's why the author spends a good bit of space in this book dealing with many of those additives that dilute the Gospel. The goal is not to pick fights over doctrinal points. It is much more practical than that. By clearing away the clusters of what's untrue in your belief system, the readers' attention will be freed up to focus on what's true, and then their faith will be able to rest on a good and pure foundation. And then, in the words of Jesus, you can really know (i.e., fully experience) the truth, and the truth shall set you free.

A quick disclaimer: I am not a medical professional. Therefore, what I wrote in this foreword is not medical advice and it should not be construed as such in any way. With that said, the book that you are holding in your hands is one of the best resources I've come across on the subject of divine healing. I hope you enjoy reading it as much as I did.

~Oleg Aristo

PREFACE

Every book is a new experience. This one was no different. After ministering to people over the phone, I found myself changing the way I presented healing, noticing things that they were now understanding, but also things where they still had misperceptions about. What started out as a follow up book to "Unlocking the Mystery of Divine Healing" turned out to be a book with an even greater depth of information on how to receive healing. What I had thought was going to be a simple walk through of how I minister to others turned out to be much deeper on information.

There is such a need for healing within the body of Christ that there is a need for us as leaders to share the revelations Holy Spirit has given us. I cannot rest until every person actively seeking healing has attained it, for themselves. Then, they pass that blessing on to others until the body of Christ is whole. It will be then we can focus on pulling in unbelievers through healing as well.

It was a phone conversation with a friend that inspired this book. He just needed a few gentle nudges to see his body healthy. That conversation that gave me the nudge that was needed for me to share more of my knowledge on healing.

My style of writing is born from being a better verbal communicator than writer. As I'm writing, I'm pretending that the reader is directly in front of me and I'm really carrying on a conversation. Be forewarned! This is the way that comes naturally to me.

This does include topics approached that cause me to have a righteous anger. Just as in a conversation, you will be able to spot those topics that I am extremely passionate about. Keep this in mind, as you read. My anger on these topics is not directed towards any specific person, rather on the trash traditions that have been taught. These teachings and mindsets that keep people sick.

Read with an open heart and open mind. My prayers is that, while reading, you are able to acknowledge your healing. Be blessed, be healed, and be a blessing.

1 MINDING THE FLESH

We have Adam and Eve in paradise. They grab the fruit of the tree of Knowledge of Good and Evil. A few bites and they are removed from the garden. Death and it's causes then entered the world. **Warning: This is my summary of what happened.** The purpose of these first few chapters is to explain the struggle of being healed. Looking at the past helps to understand the whole view of healing. The question of why healing appears so difficult to achieve will be answered in these first few chapters. Have a full pot of coffee ready, sit back, contemplate, and allow the eyes of your understanding be opened. We're going back to the garden for a bit so that a full understanding of what Paul meant in the following scripture, can be attained:

> *For they that are after the flesh do mind the things of the flesh; but they that are after the spirit the things of the Spirit. For to be carnally minded is death; but to be spiritually minded is life and peace. Because the carnal mind is enmity against God: for it is not subject to the law of God, neither indeed can be. (Romans 8:5-7, King James Bible)*

Let's talk about trees. We've got the tree of Life and then there's the tree of knowledge of good and evil. Did God cause the tree of knowledge of good and evil to exist? That is the first question.

Moses, the writer of Genesis, wasn't there and didn't know Adam.

When Moses was writing Genesis, he viewed God as both good and evil because of Adam eating from the tree of knowledge. During Moses time, the world was under the Kingdom of darkness and Moses did not have the Holy Spirit. His perception of God was off, and we see many examples of that in scripture. I don't want to belabor this, but I think it is an important reminder. Here is one:

> *And out of the ground made the Lord God to grow every tree that is pleasant to the sight, and good for food; the tree of life also in the midst of the garden, and the tree of knowledge of good and evil. (Genesis 2:9)*

The Father of all that is good did undoubtedly cause the tree of Life to grow. There is no questioning that. However, there is a question of whether He had caused the tree of knowledge of good and evil to grow. "Take a deep breath and just have an open heart on this matter". I question this because of what James, a Holy Spirit filled Apostle, writes:

> *Let no man say when he is tempted, I am tempted of God: for God cannot be tempted with evil, neither tempteth he any man... Every good gift and every perfect gift is from above, and cometh down from the Father of lights, with whom is no variableness, neither shadow of turning. (James 1:13,17)*

If God had caused that tree to grow, then he would've been tempting Adam. Not only that, but according to James, only good gifts come from God. Therefore, is it in God's nature to create something that would cause His creation such devastation? **I think not!**

There is no variation with Our Father. I believe that the tree grew because the serpent caused Adam to speak words to cause this tree to grow. God had given Adam authority over the world. God then warned Adam to not eat of it. The serpent had knowledge of the tree, so the serpent knew that the tree was there and that God hath said not to eat from it. The serpent had been in the garden since the animals were created. Anyhow, this is just food for thought.

Next, the serpent draws Eve's attention to the tree. Take note of this. The serpent takes advantage of Eve's physical senses. Up to this point, Adam and Eve only used their physical senses to interact with the world. Their physical senses did not overwhelm them. They were not controlled by what they saw, until they ate of the fruit and then their eyes were opened.

It was at this point the carnal mind (the visually sensitive, logical brain) was born. The brain was caused to come alive subject to our physical senses. Now is that point in time that it took over. It is through the control center of the physical senses that the physical nature of things enter in.

Paul is not referring to a persons unrenewed mind or the soul because the soul is subject to the law of God. This is huge to understand. We are our spirit and our soul. We are not our brain.

The brain came alive, then they noticed that they were naked. They had been naked all along, but before they ate the fruit, they had no recognition of it. They had been walking in the spirit, which is life and peace. Now, suddenly their brain became awakened and they started walking by sight. They saw they were naked, became ashamed, and hid. They decided to be ashamed and hide because, for the first time, they became reliant on their physical senses. This is the reason that Paul states that we do not walk by sight.

A side note but a very important note: What did the serpent use to entice Eve? That's right food! Since that day in the garden what has man's life been based around? That is correct, food.

Without the original sin, man's first desire would've been relationship with their Creator. Yes, they would have eaten and enjoyed food. It was created by God for our pleasure. But interaction with God would have been the primary purpose of life.

I will also state it isn't food that is evil. Food should be neutral. However, the importance we place on food is where we use it for evil. This will come as a shock to many, but originally, it wasn't food that sustained life. It was God's spirit within us. His very breath.

The fall happened, and His breath was removed from us. Then, we became reliant upon food to sustain life. Take a deep breath! It's going to be ok. This will become an important concept to grasp.

Who's the Bread of Life? Yes, Jesus! Who then sustains us? Not what we put into mouths, but the very spirit of Life: Holy Spirit within us. Ponder on this while we continue to move forward and relax. Remember, this is coming from a person that was sustained six months with no food.

Continuing with our journey, without God's Spirit being joined with Adam & Eve's spirits, they became susceptible to pain, injury, and sickness. The human brain was being programmed. The input was coming from the physical world, through the physical senses. The further in time from the garden the less memory their spirit had from the time of the garden.

It wasn't man's spirit that died in the garden. Rather, it was God's spirit being removed from their spirit. They no longer had His sustaining life within them. They became reliant on the physical things. The brain started to recall physical experiences and store them to be passed along throughout generations. For instance, hit a man in the head with a rock. Blood pours out, his skull is crushed, and he's dead. A physical action equals a physical result. In other words, *Romans 8:5 says, "Those who are after the flesh do mind the things of the flesh"* which results in death.

Since God's Spirit was no longer in them, the spiritual truths became a thing of the ever growing, distant past. Therefore, the physical world ruled. Man's foundation of truth became what they saw. A blemish on the skin became leprosy and men died. People would notice if you touched this plant, a rash would appear. Eat of that plant and you would drop dead. This became the normal and is what man's wisdom is. This wisdom is based purely on the seen world. If you do this, this is what will happen.

Through time this is what came to be expected. Man had become mortal. Even though man had been given authority over the physical world, few recognized or used it. I am talking about the B.C. Days. Those who did recognize that mankind had authority over the Earth, used it to attain the only pleasures this world had which boils down to food and sex. By the way, the food that was eaten in those days was not the food that God originally created. It was a corrupted version. So those that claim, "God created this type of food, so that's what we should eat," are wrong. They are sadly mistaken. Everything was corrupted.

As I stated, there were those who recognized, "In Adam," man had authority over animals and the natural world. They used that authority to do what appeared as "supernatural". That is what sorcery and witchcraft are about. It is the use of our God given, natural authority over the world. This was used for evil, to attain wealth and fame.

All of this came about because the physical senses were relied upon to determine cause and effect, the "natural order of things." Mankind determined cause and effect based upon what they saw. They had completely forgotten the days of the garden of Eden.

> *Wherefore, as by one man sin entered into the world, and death by sin; and so death passed upon all men, for that all have sinned: (For until the law, sin was in the world. but sin is not imputed when there is no law). Nevertheless, death reigned from Adam to Moses, even over them that had not sinned, after the similitude of Adam's transgression, who is a figure of him that was to come. (Romans 5:12-14)*

Unlike Adam and Eve, the rest of mankind had not directly eaten of the Tree of Knowledge of Good and Evil. Yet, since it had awakened the logical brain, they suffered the consequences because all mankind knew at that point, the cause and effect. What they saw was coming in from the physical world. The world was filled with darkness because that is all mankind knew. This was not God punishing the world. Understand this. God was not punishing the world. It was not He that was causing death because God was not holding man accountable for their individual evils. It was not God abandoning mankind. Rather, it was the cause and effect of the physical world causing mankind to be unable to hear God. They were overwhelmed by their physical senses.

There were demons yelling in mankind's ears. Demons are spiritual beings that carry lies. Directing man's path to evil absolutely. This was the same way the serpent had done with Eve. Just like Eve they were susceptible to the lies. Demons contain no power other than lies and deceit.

It is through mankind's natural authority that demons work. The devil or demons never had the ability to cause things to happen. The way things happen is by finding a person that will listen, that will allow them to use a person's natural authority. It was that way with the serpent. He used subtlety to get Eve to perform his wishes. He could not force Eve to do anything.

The way evil works in this world is accomplished not by demons or Satan's supernatural abilities, but through man's authority. They get things done by lies, deceit, through vain imaginations, and evil speaking's. Then, because a human spoke it, things happen. It isn't from any authority that demons have. We'll talk more about that later. If I hit you with too much information, you'll get overwhelmed. I don't want that. Some of you got left behind with the first paragraph, probably still calling that heresy.

Some may be scratching their heads wondering, "What does this all have to do with healing?" If all that we know is the things of the physical world, the only way it can end is by death. From Adam to Moses after the fall that is all they knew, the physical things of this world. This is where we get that if we're searching for the physical truth of this world by relying on our physical senses, then all we will get is death. Another way to put this is, if I'm searching for the solution to a problem through the physical realities, then the only answer we will see is the physical truth: which ends in death.

This path has existed since Cain, he could see nothing, except the physical plane. This was the reason he killed Abel. It also included all the gentile nations. Even within the nation of Israel itself, there were those that only saw the physical nature of things, discounting the spiritual truths of the Earth. This was most of the nation of Israel. While claiming God as theirs, they could only recognize The Law of Moses. Today, there are still those that only recognize the physical truths.

A good example is that after Christ's Resurrection, for roughly one thousand years, miracles did abound. Then, mankind grew in medicine and knowledge. They stopped associating healing with Christ. Knowledge grew, yes, the wisdom of men. They began to associate healing with herbs and certain foods. Take this and it will heal you, rub this on a wound and it will disinfect the wound. Because mankind was once again looking at the physical world through their physical senses. Those who seek after the flesh will find those things. If you're looking at a problem with the carnal mindset, you may find a physical solution. But the result will always lead to death.

2 DAYS OF OLD

We made it to chapter two. That's fantastic! Do you have a fresh pot of coffee? We looked at "the flesh," how after the infamous bite of the fruit the physical senses overwhelmed mankind. They only knew what was coming in through their physical senses. Now, let's look at the spiritual side of things. Starting with Adam, the world was in darkness. Satan was the ruler through the physical senses of man.

Yet, God never gave up on mankind. He went searching to and fro to find a person that could still hear Him. Let's look at the part of Romans about they are after the spirit, the things of the Spirit, which are life and peace.

> *For they that are after the flesh do mind the things of the flesh; but they that are after the spirit the things of the Spirit. For to be carnally minded is death; but to be spiritually minded is life and peace. Because the carnal mind is enmity against God: for it is not subject to the law of God, neither indeed can be. (Romans 8:5-7)*

Relying on our spiritual mind is life and peace. God did not abandon the human race! He went searching for those that could hear Him. Just like with the dark side of things, God had to work through a person of flesh and blood to achieve His Will.

Yet, while the dark forces relied upon man's natural authority only,

God would give spiritual authority to those who heard Him. The ones who heard God were much fewer than those who relied only on their physical senses. But from Adam to Moses, these people who heard and served God, lived longer and were prosperous.

Yet, because of the awakening of their physical senses, they were still susceptible to hearing from the world and God. It was a back and forth struggle. God created a means of escape, so He could rescue all His Creation. He then chose Abraham to keep a people connected to Him. Abraham is the Father of our faith, prior to the Law of Moses. It is through Abraham that we have the promise, which by the way is The Holy Spirit.

> *That the blessing of Abraham might come on the Gentiles through Jesus Christ; that we might receive the promise of the Spirit through Faith....Now to Abraham and his seed were the promises made. He saith not, And to seeds, as of many; but as of one, and to thy seed, which is Christ. (Galatians 3:14, 16)*

I get many of you know this. But what I need to show is the reason why God chose Abraham. He had to keep those that could hear Him together so that Jesus could be spoken into existence.

There were two things operating at the same time. Those that lived only by their physical senses (Gentiles), and those who could live by the Spirit. But at this point, the Holy Spirit was outside of them just as Satan or the world was. Abraham and his descendants would hear both voices. Abraham heard God vaguely and would mix up the voice of God with the voice of this world which is how Ishmael came about before Isaac. Ishmael is the example of operating from the physical senses. While Isaac is the example of being born from the Spirit, two things operating both in the physical world with two separate paths.

Moses and the children of Israel. Take a breath. God used His servant Moses to operate through. This kept spiritual truths operating in the world. Remember that He had given man authority over all things on the Earth. All the miracles performed through Moses were a reminder of what Adam and Eve had in the garden. Through all of this, God kept this now faded memory alive, the remembrance of how to operate from the spirit. The Hebrews show how God sustains us. Up until the Law of Moses, there wasn't one feeble person among them. The manna coming down from the sky, all the miracles of that time, all of these were to maintain the remembrance of where mankind was and to what was to come, which is total restoration.

The Loving Father did not leave the Earth because of the original sin nor did He abandon mankind. Yet, through Israel He showed what has now come. He was sustaining Israel providing for all their needs. This was even though Holy Spirit no longer resided within man. The spiritual truth of things is always directly upon the Earth, but at this time it existed outside of man, one plane, two different paths which directly affect the physical world. Take note of this distinction. There's a reason for this distinction. God is a spirit He created the world through the spirit of His Word. The physical does not exist without the spiritual. The spiritual does exist without the physical.

> *Through faith we understand that the worlds were framed by the word of God, so that the things which were seen were not made of things which do appear. (Hebrews 11:3)*

Underneath the physical thing, outside of sight, is the spiritual reality. What makes things seen is present and flowing. That is the real substance of things. We can take things at face value which is what is seen through the physical senses, "living by the flesh," or we can recognize the true reality of things, "the spiritual mind" or the mind of Christ, which was not available at the time of Moses.

Therefore, God set up the Law of Moses to show the children of Israel what was good and pure. Remember that all men understood were the physical things. This law was set to show the spiritual truth.

During the period of the Law of Moses, there was still both the physical operating and the spiritual. While Moses was alive, things went reasonably well for the children of Israel because Moses had a sense of spirituality. After that, the physical senses did rule. But the line of spirituality was running through the nation by individuals that could still hear God.

These were the prophets, which through whom came the prophecies, the spoken word. They spoke Jesus into existence. That is really what all the prophecies were about, speaking Christ into existence. I could really get deep on this topic. For Christ to be born of a woman, by the seed of Holy Spirit, man had to speak it out just as Moses had to part his arms for the red sea to separate, hit the rock for water to pour out, throw his staff on the ground and the many other miracles that occurred.

Most of the leadership saw the Laws of Moses not as a means for God to show what righteousness is, but strict unbendable laws meant for punishment. They could not see the spiritual significance. Also, throughout the Old Covenant there were healings showing us that mortal life is important to God. But there were four things that the Levitical priesthood could not see healed: Those lame from birth, leprosy, deaf mute spirits (which included the blind), and people raised from the dead after seventy-two hours. These signs were spoken by God to Moses to being able to identify the Messiah. More about that later.

All of those who were under the Law of Moses saw God as both good and evil. That was because of the fruit of the tree of Good and evil. A duplicity of man had been born as of the crunch, crunch of the fruit. It wasn't God that had changed, but man's way of observing Him.

Throughout this time within the children of Israel there were those who kept themselves for God even while misinterpreting what God was saying. The devil was speaking to them at the same time, not one person alive at the time had a true perception of God. Not Moses, not Joshua, not even the prophets. Here's what Jesus said in the book of John:

Then said Jesus unto them again, Verily, verily, I say unto you, I am the door of the sheep. All that ever came before me are thieves and robbers: but the sheep did not hear them. (10:7-10) I and my Father are one. (10:30) If I do not the works of my Father, believe me not. But if I do, though ye believe not me, believe the works: that ye may know, and believe, that the Father is in me, and I in him. (10:37-38) No one has ever seen God. But the unique One, who is himself God, is near to the Father's heart. He has revealed God to us.(John 1:18, NLT)

Jesus, because He was born of the Holy Spirit, was the only person alive that really knew the Father. He alone was not affected by the fruit of the tree of Eden. Jesus did not rely on his physical senses, nor did he see God as both good and evil. 'I also want to point out the works that I do,' was Jesus referring to the four miracles only the Messiah could perform.

The verses above are huge. They show the only correct representation of the Father is the Son. Everyone else, was hearing from the world and from God. One minute they were hearing correctly the next minute not. All of this is important when trying to understand healing. The Apostles themselves during the Old Covenant, which they were a part of before the cross, would hear from Jesus, not understand, and listen to the physical senses instead. Peter, when Jesus rebuked him saying, "get thee behind me Satan," is a perfect example.

Jesus turned to Peter and said, "Get away from me Satan! You are a dangerous trap to me. You are seeing things merely from a human point of view, not from God's." (Matthew 16:23, NLT)

Peter was seeing things from his physical senses, not from the "mind of Christ". Because at that time Jesus hadn't gone to the Cross, He was still ruled by his physical senses and the world coming through them. We often make the mistake of looking back through the Old Testament Scriptures without realizing the huge difference between then and now. We take King David, Moses, and yes even the Prophets and place them as knowing God better than us. We have the 'mind of Christ,' they did not.

The four Gospels were Old Covenant, Christ was fulfilling all the Old Covenant prophecies. We take the individual healings and pick them apart to discover secrets about healing. This is a huge mistake. Therefore, we only get to a certain level of healing and no farther. We limit ourselves and the body of Christ by doing this. We also come to many wrong conclusions, because we do this. **Please listen to this!**

> *Verily, verily, I say unto you, He that believeth on me, the works that I do shall he do also; and greater works than these shall he do; because I go unto my Father. (John 14:12)*

Remember the mention of the four miracles that only the Messiah could perform? Set aside those that Jesus stated ye of great faith. Set those individual healings aside. All the other individual accounts were the four miracles only the Messiah could perform. **They aren't in scripture for us to develop theologies on healing from. NO!**

This misunderstanding is what is limiting the Modern-Day Body of Christ from living as we were meant to live. Jesus performed them to prove that He was indeed the Messiah. When Jesus came on the scene at first, He alone performed these individual accounts of healing. The Levitical priesthood, and the other religious orders of the day were performing miracles as well.

What set Jesus apart were what was healed. That is why the crowds were amazed and the Pharisees flabbergasted. Let's start off with John the Baptist. When imprisoned, he sent his disciples to Jesus not from a lack of faith, it was from faith. He was asking for the proof of the four miracles. That's why Jesus took the disciples of John around and showed them what healings were happening.

> *Now when John had heard in the prison the works of Christ, he sent two of his disciples, and said unto him, Art thou he that should come, or do we look for another? Jesus answered and said unto them, Go and shew John again those things which ye do hear and see: The blind receive their sight, and the lame walk, the lepers are cleansed, and the deaf hear, the dead are raised up, and the poor have the gospel preached to them. (Matthew 11:2-5, KJV)*

Those things had never been done before. The priests of the day would not even pray for the blind, lame from birth, leprosy, the deaf, and the dead after three days! That's why the crowds were amazed, and the Pharisees infuriated.

> *And Jesus put forth his hand, and touched him, saying, I will; be thou clean. And immediately his leprosy was cleansed. And Jesus saith unto him, See thou tell no man; but go thy way, shew thyself to the priests, and offer the gift that Moses commanded,* **for a testimony unto them**. *(Matthew 8:3-4, KJV)*

Moses had enacted the law of the priests determining if a leper had been cleansed. No Jew had ever been cleansed before. Miriam had been healed, before they came under the Law of Moses. She wasn't a Jew at the time. Jesus points this out to the Pharisees in another instance. This was enacted purely to prove Jesus was the Christ. Until Matthew 10, Jesus was fulfilling the four miracles.

Then when the Pharisees accused Jesus of casting Satan out of Satan, that was the Pharisees denying the Holy Spirit because those miracles were specifically for Jesus. In accusing Him, they condemned themselves. After this, was when Jesus elected the twelve and then the seventy to heal the sick, raise the dead, and so forth. At that time the priests could no longer heal. The transition was starting to happen. Jesus put off going to Lazarus, because he was the final miracle that proved Jesus was the Messiah, the dead raised after three days. That is why the pharisees wanted Lazarus dead. Yet, we want to make theologies out of it!

These were miracles performed for a very specific reason, to prove that Jesus was the Christ. **Quit coming up with wrong theologies! Just stop doing it already! Our examples of what healing should look like come after Christ's resurrection: Peter and his shadow, Paul and his cloth, etc.**

There is a lot more I could cover about those four miracles. In every instance there is much I could write to fully prove it even further. Suffice it to say it's best for you study it out for yourself. The game changer is after Jesus' resurrection. He brought the Kingdom of God to Earth for the first time. Nothing looks the same after the cross!

3 GODS SPIRIT IN MAN

How's the coffee going down? I was able to roast some more yesterday. Thank You Jesus!

The first three chapters are a summary of what had transpired before Jesus' resurrection. The focus is on healing. But along the way, I needed to share my point of view on things. This chapter is a look at things that may seem weird to you. As always, study it out for yourself. Okay, we got talk about the Cross to clear up a whole bunch of misconceptions.

This may offend many of you. Why? It is because of the way you were taught, that God had to punish sin. Therefore, since sin is in the body God had to take his wrath out on Jesus. That my dear friends is where the misconception starts. This is where the duality comes in. Because of the fruit of the tree of good and evil, man became good and evil, **not** God. Mankind looked at God as being both good and evil. What the Father had to do was to take the effects of the fruit out of this world. This is what Jesus was born to do.

Remember until Moses, there was death and sickness. This was the effect of the fruit, not God's punishment. We look at it as God's punishment. It wasn't. All the evil of the world was because of the effect of the fruit.

> *Wherefore as by one man sin entered into the world, and death by sin; and so death passed upon all*

> *men, for that all have sinned: (until the law sin was in the world but sin is not imputed when there is no law). Nevertheless, death reigned from Adam to Moses, even over them that had not sinned, after the similitude of Adam's transgression, who is a figure of him that was to come. (Romans 5:12-14, KJV)*

Look at it like this: If someone gave me something that caused me to go crazy, I would be put into a mental institution for my safety and others safety. They would then get the poison out of me, but would I be accountable for my actions during the time I was poisoned? In a perfect world no, I wouldn't be. This is how The Father looks at mankind.

There was a poison put into us. The whole world went nuts. The Father didn't hold mankind responsible, so He didn't put sin on us. The effects of the poison were still there. So, in order for full restoration, the poison had to be sucked out. In order for the poison to be sucked out, there had to be an uncontaminated vessel. This vessel had to be pure, so the poison wouldn't escape.

The perfect vessel was Jesus. He sucked the poison into His body so that the original poison was now in His Body. By dying He took the poison out of this world. Where is the wrath of God on Jesus at the Cross? Why then would the Father forsake the Son? He wouldn't and didn't.

> *Behold, the hour cometh, yea, is now come, that ye shall be scattered, every man to his own, and shall leave me alone: and yet I am not alone, because the Father is with me. (John 16:32, KJV)*

That is the first thing accomplished at the Cross: Jesus took the original poison out of the world. The second thing was as follows. God separated the children of Israel and set forth the Law of Moses for two reasons: 1) These were the people that could hear Him, although vaguely and sporadically, and 2) to show everyone the world was infected. He worked through those within Israel that could hear him, to speak Christ into existence and as proof of what was happening. The other group within the Children of Israel was to expose the fact that all the world was infected. He set down the Laws. If they could follow all the Laws, then they were not infected, so then no antidote for the rest of the world was needed. If they could not follow the laws, then they were infected therefore not held liable.

What the Father did was isolate a group of people like a scientist would isolate a control group if they were test subjects (for lack of a better description). The Father already knew the outcome of the test but had to be able to prove it to the world. This is what the Law of Moses was all about.

Within that group of people, He implanted the cure in one person. That person would be Christ Jesus, the cure is Holy Spirit. That person had to be able to live just like everyone else, be among them, and not become infected. Just like a scientist would "prove" a cure, the person would have to undergo every test and live exactly like those infected to show that he was indeed cured. By doing so He vindicated the entire world.

While at the same time, because the test subjects (Israel) had been placed in a special environment, three things happened at the Cross: 1) Christ took into His Body the original poison (the fruit), 2) He took the sins of Israel into His Own Body, and 3) He broke down the special environment the Children of Israel had been put in, in other words, The Law of Moses. At the Cross these were all the things that Christ took into His Body, the only pure vessel that could contain the original sin, diseases, death and the sins of Israel. This had to happen in order for the entire world to have the cure. He literally took all of these conditions out of the world, into hell, and came back fully restored. The whole world was now ready for the cure. That which had kept men from seeing the Pure Goodness of God had been taken away.

Ok, I hear ya. Now a whole lot of man's wisdom is pouring in. What about this certain scripture? What about that certain scripture? What keeps us from being able to understand this is the traditions and wisdom of men. You can believe this or not, theologians try to prove point by points. I'm giving the full scope of things, so all can understand. It's up to you to accept or reject.

What I have to prove is that the New Covenant is completely outside and apart from the Law of Moses. It was completely completed and was only set in place for the reasons I described. This is what all the Epistles of Paul were about. Jesus preached the Good News of God's Kingdom coming to Earth. Paul's mission and gospel was the cure, Christ Jesus.

Let's back track so we can move forward. There's a bunch of walls I gotta take down with my trusty sledgehammer. Did I mention that this book is taking a direction that I hadn't thought I was going to take? Let's take a coffee break!

This is going to show how much legalism and churchiness is in each and every one of us, my friends. You obviously are not that churchy to have made it this far. You must be seeking Truth. All I can say is, "Lord Jesus Help me!"

The children of Israel were separated from the rest of the world to this point. The cure who is Christ Jesus was as well. The biggest error we make is placing Jesus in the year 2018 and thinking that what He said applied to us, as if He were speaking directly to us today. Jesus was born under the Law and sent to a people under the Law. We must then understand who He was speaking to and His original intent in what He was stating. Today we have the Holy Spirit. They didn't. Today we're in the New Covenant. They weren't. We don't dismiss any of His Words, but we have to put them in proper perspective.

Setting the gentiles aside, they were not imputed with sin, at this point. They were entirely separate, they had no salvation or hope. They lived life purely in the kingdom of darkness. They had no law. So, where there is no law, there is no sin. Yet, they were entirely subject to the darkness. Which is why there were false gods.

Jesus on His earthly mission was only here for the Children of Israel. So, the words He spoke were only for them. Matthew says:

> *These twelve Jesus sent forth, and commanded them saying, go not into the way of the Gentiles, and into any city of the Samaritans enter ye not: But go rather to the lost sheep of the house of Israel. And as ye go, preach, saying, the kingdom of heaven is at hand. (Matthew 10:5-7, KJV)*

For us in 2018, the Kingdom of heaven is in us! There is an application, but we must understand how to take Jesus' words. He also states do not go into the way of the Gentiles, that doesn't apply to us today, proper perspective. He had only come for the lost sheep of Israel. All of Israel was lost:

> *But he answered and said, I am not sent but unto the lost sheep of the house of Israel." (Matthew 15:24, KJV)*

He wasn't sent on His earthly ministry for anyone but those who were quarantined. He was laying the foundation for the Kingdom of God. Think of it like this, the automobile has already been invented. So why in the world would I use a blue print from the very first model T? I can't dismiss the blue print and say it's false, but I do have to put it in its proper place. It was the foundation for building a car. We've advanced far past that.

We do have the entire Bible to learn from but must handle it in its proper perspective. What we try to do is take the blue print from the model T and the blueprint from a 2018 Ford and use both at the same time which creates confusion and probably a vehicle that won't even function. It's the same way with God's Kingdom.

Jesus was speaking to those prior to the Cross, His Resurrection, and prior to Pentecost. We are past those days which is exactly what His statements about the new and old wine skins were about.

Jesus being the vessel for the cure, was preparing Israel for the cure. He was getting them to understand why the Law was implemented. Fast forward to His Resurrection. It was here that He now states:

> *And he said unto them, go ye into all the world, and preach the gospel to every creature." (Mark 16:15)*

After His resurrection is when this happened. Jesus was now to take His place at the right hand of the Father. Now is when the barrier was taken down. This is when Jesus was fulfilling that which he had spoken:

> *And other sheep I have, which are not of this fold: them also I must bring, and they shall hear my voice; and there shall be one fold, and one shepherd. (John 10:16)*

As of the Resurrection, the Old Covenant was no longer in force. Yet, the Jews continued in it. God set forth a time period of transition. We have the day of Pentecost which was step one.

God poured out His Spirit on all flesh. Now came the period of enlightenment. With the day of Pentecost, the Cure was poured out! We at that moment became the Temple of the Holy Spirit. Two things were still operating at the same time: those of the Spirit and those of the LAW of Moses.

Those who minded the Words of the Holy Spirit reaped Life and Peace. Those that minded the physical senses and those of the world and the physical laws of man would reap death. The Old Covenant was no longer in effect. So, those who put themselves under it were under the Law of Man, not under God's Kingdom. With the day of Pentecost, we are one-fold with one shepherd. There is not the Jew on one hand and the Christians on the other hand. Christ pulled us all unto Himself. Paul was set apart to teach us the Gospel of Christ along with the other Apostles. Here are some examples:

> *For he is our peace, who hath made both one, and hath broken down the middle wall of partition between us. Having abolished in his flesh the enmity, even the law of commandments contained in ordinances, for to make in himself of twain one new man, so making peace; (Ephesians 2:14-15)*

> *There is neither Jew nor Greek, there is neither bond nor free, there is neither male nor female: for ye are all one in Christ Jesus. (Galatians 3:28)*

This is not a future event this happened over two thousand years ago. With the Cure Poured out, it was Truth even back then. Since the Law of Moses was fulfilled, our history goes directly to God's Promise to Abraham which was the promise of the Holy Spirit. Paul explains this in Galatians:

> *That the blessing of Abraham might come on the Gentiles through Jesus Christ; that we might receive the promise of the Spirit through faith.... Now to Abraham and his seed were the promises made. He saith not, and to seeds, as of many; but as of one, and to thy seed, which is Christ. (3:14,16)*

This is the spiritual truth that runs concurrent with the physical reality. Mankind now has the Holy Spirit inside of them who is giving life to our mortal bodies. Holy Spirit is speaking to us saying we are healed. The legalistic mentality or the mind of Adam, is focused on the physical realities that is coming in through the physical senses. The mind of Christ within us is saying that we are now sons of God. We, right now, have access to living miraculously. We are actually fully restored. The reasons why we aren't seeing this lived out, are coming up.

Paul was handpicked by Christ, to preach the Gospel of Christ. It is by his revelations that we are to live life in the New Covenant out, to a point. He is a starting point. Paul's revelations just as Jesus' were for a specific time period. This is what Christianity keeps missing:

> *In the day when God shall judge the secrets of men by Jesus Christ according to my gospel. (Romans 2:16)*
>
> *Now to him that is of power to establish you according to my gospel, and the preaching of Jesus Christ, according to the revelation of the mystery, which was kept secret since the world began. (Romans 16:25)*
>
> *Remember that Jesus Christ of the seed of David was raised from the dead according to my gospel: (2 Timothy 2:8)*
>
> *From henceforth let no man trouble me: for I bear in my body the marks of the Lord Jesus. (Galatians 6:17)*

Paul more than anyone was charged with the Gospel of Christ. It was from this Gospel that the men of that time would be judged. This was a time of miracles for there were two gospels. Jesus preached the Gospel of the Kingdom of God, this was the preparatory Gospel. Paul preached the gospel of Christ, along with the other Apostles. For roughly thirty-six years the gospel of Christ was preached. Then came the end of the age of the Old Covenant.

Miracles abounded. First, Paul preached to the gentiles. Then, he ended up preaching to the Jews in Rome. The destruction of the Temple of Jerusalem was the end of the nation of Israel. The war of the Jews ended around 73 A.D. The Jews were scattered and for roughly a thousand years what came to be known as Christianity thrived. This was the purest time in Christianity until around 1300 A.D. when religion reared its ugly head once again. The Name of Christ was still heard, but mankind went back to relying on their physical senses.

> *For he that soweth to his flesh shall of the flesh reap corruption, but he that soweth to the Spirit*

shall of the Spirit reap life everlasting." (Galatians 6:8)

During the time period from the 1300s on, mankind had stopped living in the miraculous. Yet, miracles were happening. The sacrifice of Christ was still working. People would have symptoms, eat something, then attribute what they ate to be the healer. Christ's sacrifice was healing people, but people misconstrued it to be plants. Their expectation became focused on what went in through the mouth or the salve that was made. The spiritual was still happening, but the source was misrepresented. Instead of looking at the Sacrifice of Christ and Jesus being the healer, food became the healer. Then medicines were created. This then became the normal line of thought. This is human wisdom to the point where people believe that God created medicine through man.

We rationalize this, because we've been so indoctrinated to mind the things of the physical nature. The end result is people die when that doesn't have to be. People suffer when that doesn't have to be.

4 OLD WAYS GONE

UGH! Unknown to you I've restarted this book four times! The way that it was going to be written has changed. Excuse me while I drink a whole pot of coffee.

We are coming out of Religion. For some nine hundred years, those who ruled only by the strict coherence to the Law were ruling, telling people what to think. In my words, the ones ruling only understood what was being taught through the physical nature of things. We are coming to know the mind of Christ through relationship once again. What confuses us is that we are trying to understand Christianity through scriptures without having the full scope of what had happened.

Just as Jesus (until His Resurrection), came only for those born under the Law. Paul was chosen by Christ to show the gentiles and the Jews the Gospel of Christ. Just like with Jesus, we can't dismiss anything that he wrote. But we must take it in the proper perspective. Jesus was the model T, Paul is a 1967 Stingray corvette. Yet, there has been advances to the car since even then. The same way we have Jesus who taught on the Kingdom of God, Paul had the Gospel of Christ. We can't stop there. Things have advanced further. Those two foundations remain true, but there's more truth added to it now.

Jesus laid out the foundation, set the concrete which Paul built upon. He framed Christianity. Then, after the end of the age, (The End of the Law of Moses), others came and lived out Christianity being entirely free from religion. We don't have the knowledge of that time period, it isn't in our Bibles! When we read Paul saying things like,

> *In that he saith, A new covenant, he hath made the first old. Now that which decayeth and waxeth old is ready to vanish away. (Hebrews 8:13)*

We get the wrong perception that we are still waiting for something to grow old and vanish away. It already did vanish away, it was the Law of Moses. The Jews had kept the standards of the Old Covenant from Christ's death on for roughly thirty-six years. Until the destruction of Jerusalem in 70 A.D. Then it was completely wiped off the face of this Earth. I'm not going try to explain all of this right now. Then we have men rushing in and forming religion.

Where does this leave us in the year 2018? Most of us it leaves confused, misguided, frustrated, and eager to experience true Christianity. Healing has been revived. But many are still lost with a bunch of wrong beliefs about healing which is brought about by the mixture of the religious teachings and what we've experienced on this Earth to the present time. All of the previous chapters were to show the history, so we can understand where and why we're at the place we're at. With Adam, we lost the Holy Spirit living within us and became infected with relying only on our physical senses. That was restored within us on the Day of Pentecost, and we became a new man. We were reborn, and capable of everything that Jesus was capable of and more. Then, in the history of mankind, we lost that knowledge because of religious teaching. We returned back to relying on our physical senses and not on the mind of Christ. At present, we are relearning that which was lost. That is Who we truly are In Christ, the Apostles knew and lived out. Now, we need to surpass them. We can do this because they have set the example and move forward past even their understanding.

In "Unlocking the Mystery of Divine Healing," I broke healing down into a simple formula that we believe, expect, and then we can acknowledge that we are healed. I also showed how the control center called the brain controls what we see in our physical bodies and that is the main block that keeps us from recognizing our healing. I always work from the Truth that,

> *Who his own self bare our sins in his own body on the tree, that we, being dead to sins, should live unto righteousness: by whose stripes ye were healed. (1 Peter 2:24)*

We were already healed is the Truth that I work from. There is nothing that can block what has already happened. We have only to recognize this. Then, we can acknowledge that we are indeed healed. What is holding us back is little phrases wrongly perceived that were taken from Paul's writings. As discussed earlier, Paul's teachings were for His time period. We can still certainly use them but must do so in its proper perspective.

> *For we know that the whole creation groaneth and travaileth in pain together until now. And not only they, but ourselves also, which have the firstfruits of the Spirit, even we ourselves groan with ourselves waiting for the adoption, to wit the redemption of our body.... For whom he did foreknow, he also did predestinate to be conformed to the image of his Son that he might be, the firstborn among many brethren. (Romans 8:22-23, 29)*

We stop there not realizing that, since Paul, God has not frozen mankind in place, but has moved us closer. Jesus was the first born of many and the adoption has happened. They had received the first fruits of the Holy Spirit, but they were only the beginning. Part of the groaning that was happening was the revealing of Christ. Paul was waiting for the time when the Old Covenant would vanish, and the goats would be separated from the sheep. That happened with the destruction of the Temple of Jerusalem. Those in power trying to operate under the Law of Moses were now shown to be the goats. Those that believed in Christ, the sheep.

Whoa! Did I digress or what? Relax just wanted to show some missing pieces, let's get back to healing. Paul and the other disciples were the early church and capable of great things, now we are more mature and should be moving on to greater things.

We will move on to the greater things the more we realize the Holy Spirit is a person living inside of us. He is a part of us and He is the one giving life to our mortal bodies. What is written in the scriptures is only part one. We must now come to realize that the physical senses are what is holding us back from living as we truly should be. Christianity is just getting out from under the dark ages of religion that has ruled the world for 900 years now. We are now sons of God and have the full privileges of that.

> *But as many as received him, to them gave he power to become the sons of God, even to them that believe on his name. (John 1:12)*

That means we no longer have to be ruled by our physical senses and what the physical world says is possible. We have the Holy Spirit inside of us, so the physical laws no longer apply. The further we push the boundaries of this truth the more effective we become. The way we push past the physical senses is to start accepting this truth. As sons of God the natural laws no longer hold us bound. Now we need to be fed from the "mind of Christ" and stop letting the physical brain limit us.

> *For who hath known the mind of the Lord, that he may instruct him? But we have the mind of Christ. (1 Corinthians 2:16)*

Now, our Godly Wisdom comes from within us to the outside world, not the wisdom of man coming into us through the outside world. Push the boundaries. Yes, I must stay in the written word to stay on the correct path. But, along with that needs to come an interaction within ourselves so that the mind of Christ flows through us.

Think of it this way. A garden hose that is flowing blocks insects from getting into the hose. Turn the flowing water off then the insects can get in. This is the renewing process of the mind. To become transformed, we must keep the water turned on so that the unbelief of the world through our physical senses cannot get in.

As sons of God who are the temple of the Holy Spirit, we have access now to everything that entails. Which means, within me, the Holy Spirit is always releasing peace, joy, comfort, and health. We need only to recognize this.

> *And Christ lives within you, so even though your body will die because of sin the Spirit gives you life because you have been made right with God. The Spirit of God who raised Jesus from the dead, lives in you. And just as God raised Christ Jesus from the dead, he will give life to your mortal bodies by this same Spirit living within you. (The Bible, New Living Translation, Romans 8:10-11)*

Please take this verse literally. The Holy Spirit is giving life to your mortal body. Get an image of this.

Here's one way to think of it: I am already healed because He who is in me is giving life to my mortal body. Therefore, there has to be improvement. This is the beginning of understanding that there is no separation of the physical and spiritual world. The spiritual world is flowing underneath the physical world out of eyesight. But it is not *out there somewhere, it is within you.* This is the hardest but simplest thing to understand. To gain this understanding is to start walking in the spirit. This understanding will also help you to stop making decisions based upon your physical senses.

Life, health, peace is all flowing from within us outwardly. It is coming from the spirit of Christ, the mind of Christ, or Holy Spirit. It is not flowing from our physical senses into us. We as sons of God are now reborn to the point that it isn't what is on the outside world that sustains us, but He who is inside of us that is sustaining us.

You do realize that it was "In the first Adam" that the natural laws of the physical world apply, those laws that God explained to Adam. If we are reborn of the Spirit, then we are "In Christ." Now, these physical laws need no longer apply. We now have a new inheritance. If you want proof of that, look at Jesus before the Cross. Even though He was under the Old Covenant and fulfilling it, He had very few boundaries. Now in Him, after His Resurrection, with all His spiritual blessings, we are limited only by what we believe and expect to happen.

We now can be fed by the tree of Life who is Jesus. He is within us. Now, what Christ has attained for us is better than in the Garden of Eden, because it can't be taken away from us. We now have physical bodies only to interact with the physical world. The more we grow and mature into, the more we will discover this.

But Tony, our bodies have physical limitations. My answer to that is they do only to the point that we believe that they do. I went six months with no food, which proves my point. We are no longer dependent upon anything in the physical realm as much as we're able to believe that.

My real-life examples of what is possible include at least five times where my vehicle has occupied the same space as a tractor trailer. My vehicle and I should've been sheet metal scrapings on the side of a mountain. Instead, I ended up in front of the tractor trailers supernaturally.

I, having been healed from Lou Gehrig's disease, am a complete miracle. Part of it included going six months with no food whatsoever. My stomach was completely paralyzed with no intravenous feeding or feeding tube.

Then, A sledgehammer hit my knee full on, full force. I fell to the ground, came back up, and experienced no pain whatsoever, no bruising, nothing. My knee was absolutely fine. The list goes on:

-A man whose leg was amputated grew back.

-A woman's arm that was only ten inches long grew back.
-A sewage line that was blocked, was supernaturally unblocked.
-My phones glass cover was cracked, supernaturally repaired.
-The electricity at a pet store that was supposed to be off for hours came back on, instantly.
-A man who had refused to have emergency surgery for an appendix that had burst was suddenly healed.
-A fourteen-year-old boy who had never walked got up and walked.
-A van door that was locked with the keys locked inside was suddenly unlocked.
-My phone casing that cracked in half, which I just threw on my desk was made whole.
-A two-hour trip took only fifteen minutes.
-Two people were raised from the dead.

These are just a few examples of what, through Christ, we are capable of. These things are becoming more and more common among those who believe that nothing is impossible with God. Many of you, my friends, have seen these things as well. But this is for those of you that haven't seen or heard of these things happening. There are thousands of us walking as sons of God, who see the supernatural every single day.

5 PLUGGED INTO THE SOURCE

Yesterday, I roasted up over a pound of Cadejo coffee beans. They are my favorite beans. We now have plenty of coffee, so help yourself! Fill up a thermos if you would like to.

We get all confused because of the way we look at our history with The Father. We've looked at what was happening between the fall of man and Moses, then the days of The Law of Moses, and during that time when The Father inserted the cure, Jesus. After that, we've discussed the spreading of the Gospel of Christ with Paul. Let's break it down even further to show how we should look at healing and the supernatural things of the Kingdom of God.

> *For they that are after the flesh do mind the things of the flesh.... For to be carnally minded is death; (The Bible, King James Version, Romans 8:5a, 6a)*

We tend to separate the physical from the spiritual. This is because starting with Adam, God's Spirit was separated from our spirit. Man's spirit was still alive, but it had to rely on the physical nature of the world to feed the physical body. No longer was God's spirit feeding the body, sustaining it.

Ever wonder why God gave dominion of the world to mankind? It was in order to be able to save us. Without us having dominion of the Earth, God wouldn't have been able to use that dominion or "natural authority" to reach out to us. At this time, the spiritual world God's Kingdom was separate from the physical world. The one binding link was man's authority over the Earth. It was the link that kept us in contact with Him. This is also why we have an imagination, so that He could still connect with us, and He used it.

Satan who was the spiritual ruler of the natural world, could use it as well. But he could only use man's natural dominion. God being the creator of all things could tap into it more. Satan had no authority over anything. That is why all he can do is use man's natural authority. All demons do is tap into man's physical authority over the world through lies.

Example: Moses and Pharaoh's magicians both were able to do what we would consider "supernatural things," which was really only man's natural authority. Yet, what Moses called forth trumped the magician's abilities. Both the Heavenly Father and Satan had to reach out to man from the outside physical world through the physical senses which include the imagination.

At this point in time, everything involving man had to come from the outside physical world in. Remember, in the garden it was God's Spirit that sustained Adam and Eve. After the garden, we had to rely on food to sustain our physical bodies. In the garden food was simply used for the pleasure it wasn't the sustaining force. In the Garden there was nothing that could physically affect Adam and Eve's bodies. Their bodies were there simply to interact with the physical world. Their physical senses weren't used to keep them safe. They were completely safe and guarded from evil. After the garden, Adam and Eve had to use their physical senses to survive.

Think of it like this during the time of the Garden our bodies were like a flashlight. A flashlight is self-sustaining because its power source is a battery. Adam and Eve's bodies were self-sustaining because God's Spirit was connected to them. After the fall, they were no longer self-sustaining because they were no longer plugged into God's Spirit. Now, it was like a ceiling light bulb. Except instead of being fed from God's Spirit, now it takes a delicate design of wires running through the house and then, from the house to a main source miles away. Now they were reliant and plugged into the power plant which is the outside physical world.

The power plant being the outside world, now, the house lights are contingent on the condition of the wires running from the house to the plant. If anything happens to the wires, then there's a power outage. Not only that, but the house light is not movable it has to be permanently positioned. Furthermore, if anything happens at the power plant, if a piece of equipment blows out, then no power.

For thousands of years this is what happened due to being removed from the garden and the tree of life. Mankind's power source was the outside world. Anything that disrupted the delivery of life interfered with the human body. They were cut off from the power source of life.

The physical senses therefore became dominant. We had to learn how to spot problems with the power lines and the power source. We became susceptible to everything in the outside world. A blemish on the skin meant leprosy resulting in body pieces rotting off. An artery severed meant we bled out. We had to learn to use physical objects in order to survive. We became dependent on everything in the physical world. Man had to learn that this plant sustained life and that plant over there destroyed life. We were completely led and controlled by what we saw, our physical senses. The physical senses now, not only had to be used to survive, but through the control center, the brain, it controlled what warning signals would go off. The warning signals were swelling, bleeding, imperfect skin, pain, the many symptoms we have.

I see you're nodding your head. That's a good sign! You're agreeing with me so far. Have a cup of coffee, we're just getting warmed up.

We as Christians keep looking at the past. We see the miracles in the scriptures and we want those days not realizing we're now capable of so much more. We see the words carnal minded or flesh and we think sin. We hear the words righteous and we'll even state that Jesus made us righteous. All the while, we don't have the revelation that we are truly righteous.

There is always much talk of the Pharisees, how they couldn't see who was right in front of them. We wonder how they could not recognize who Jesus was. I want you to get what I am saying. They were carnal minded and focused only on the things of this world. Yet, even the pharisees could grasp the reality of miracles. The very same religious organization that wouldn't accept Jesus was performing miracles. The Levitical priesthood saw many miracles before and even while Jesus was in his fleshly ministry. Yet, we after Christ have trouble accepting miracles.

The reason is we separate the spiritual from the physical reality. If you're thinking that I wanted to shock you by the statement about the pharisees, you were right. Did it work?

We go about our daily routine, barely thinking about who we are In Christ. We exercise to keep our physical bodies in shape. We make sure that we are up to date on the latest news on diet. Every aspect of our daily lives is about the physical realities of the world. We were raised to be sensitive to the condition of our bodies. Our focus is set on earning a living, controlling our diet, and keeping our bodies in shape. When we cut ourselves our first thought is, "Better make sure the cut is sanitized." In fact, walk into any store today. There will be sanitizer available. We say, "God is our healer," all the while relying on food and medicines to keep us healthy. This is being carnally minded. This is making our decisions only based on the physical reality.

Jesus stated do not worry about what you shall eat or what you shall drink. All the while we're worrying about what we eat and what we drink. Yes, my friends I'm talking to you.

Granted, a lot of you are not the average Christian because you believe in healing. I see this even in the healing ministry. I hear it even from those who have seen many people healed. Some of the most physically minded people are the very ones who do see miracles. Just as the Pharisees did. Christians pride themselves on being set-apart from the rest of the world. Yet, show me how separate we are?

Think about it. How weird do you look to other people? While other people are worried about germs and putting sanitizer on their hands, are you doing the same thing? How plugged in to the physical world are you? I am not talking about "suffering for Christ" and doing without. We in this society worry about everything. How different is that from mankind in the Old Testament? This is because we separate the physical and spiritual realities in our daily lives. We think of heaven as out there or, even closer to the truth, it's a reality we'll experience when we die.

> *For whosoever will save his life shall lose it: and whosoever will lose his life for my sake shall find it. (Matthew 16:25)*

I am going to put this into a different perspective than most do. When we are so focused on surviving and taking care of our bodies, then we will lose our life. When we realize that we died in Christ and no longer have the physical boundaries that others have, then we shall find life. Think about it this way. When we are worried about everything trying to keep our bodies healthy, then we get sick. We lose the struggle. When we are outside of ourselves and showing others life and life more abundantly by showing that IN Christ we died to the physical boundaries, Christ lives in us without the boundaries of the physical nature of things than we find our life. This is exactly how my life has been.

My life before my healing, was Tony just trying to survive. The boundaries of the physical world were my prison. All I knew were the physical realities of this world. I was carnal minded. All that I saw were the physical boundaries of this world. In my case, it led to drugs, alcohol, then severe Post Traumatic Stress disorder, Lou Gehrig's disease, and bunch of other illnesses. I knew no other way to live. This was my case. Your case can be different, but it is still the same.

If you grew up in a church, then you lived trying to take care of your body and being a person of good moral character, yet, still struggling to survive in the prison of the physical reality. Then, in spite of taking good care of yourself, you became sick. Whether physically or mentally, you are still trying just to save your life. In both cases we all were locked in and dependent on the physical world.

After my healing, my eyes were opened. There is a true path beneath the surface that we have the choice to take. We can live in the spiritual reality while functioning in this physical world. While we are living in this physical world we can operate at a spiritual level, that is life and peace.

Now, I am no longer helpless when the things of this world come at me. I do not have to worry, fear or feel hopeless. The truth is, because I am In Christ, I'm a son of God which is the greatest truth, that can be known. Now, I'm no longer focused on just surviving, but living a full life. Living a full life, I'm no longer being oppressed by the physical world and am bringing others into that fullness of life.

Hopefully, you've come to understand what being carnally minded really is. We are conditioned into it, no way and no how should you feel condemned or that you're at fault. We are programmed into thinking life is about struggling to survive. That we have to make choices that are dependent upon what our physical senses are telling us.

All our lives we're told about germs, how food affects our body, better drink enough water, better exercise, better focus on the physical reality. All of these things are the wisdom of men. If you focus on the physical things, then we see the physical things. Then, death is the end result, both a physical death and spiritual death. Included in this is sin.

Once again, looking at the Pharisees, they were focused on sin and they became the biggest sinners of all. When we quit focusing on the physical nature of things and renew our minds to the Life we have In Christ, both sin and death lose their hold. We start living more sanctified lifestyles because we are no longer focused on the physical world. Our physical senses are no longer controlling our decisions. Now we can have both life and peace. I'm leaving you with these two verses. One is the problem. The other is the solution.

> *For if ye live after the flesh ye shall die: but if ye through the Spirit do mortify the deeds of the body, ye shall live. For as many as are led by the Spirit of God, they are sons of God. (Romans 8:13-14)*

6 THE FIRST BORN

We are living our lives as if Jesus has not accomplished anything! We are struggling to understand because we are like Peter before the Cross. It's the way we are taught. We cling to every word of Christ but with the understanding of Peter at that time. Really, it's how all the Apostles were before the Cross. We haven't moved past the gospels, which was the coming of God's Kingdom, into the gospel of Christ, which was Paul's Gospel, and then past that into living as sons of God. This chapter may come as a shock to many of you. Enjoy a pot of coffee, while you reflect on this verse.

> *But he turned, and said unto Peter, Get thee behind me, Satan: thou art an offense unto me: for thou savourest not the things that be of God, but those that be of men. (Matthew 16:23)*

We often think, "Peter! Peter! Don't you realize Jesus had to be sacrificed?" All the while, we are not understanding the things of God ourselves. We're living in the wisdom of men.

Peter did not know that Jesus had to offer His life so that all of us could be sons of God. He was living by the wisdom of men, knowing only the physical things of this world. Death to Peter meant finality. It was the end of Jesus, not the beginning of living life in the Kingdom of God while here on Earth.

We do the exact same thing, never coming to living in the fullness of Christ. We aren't living as sons of God. Rather, we're living as mere mortals.

Jesus is the beginning of man's integration into being sons of God. He brought the Kingdom of God to the Earth (Yes, heaven on Earth). Mankind had dominion on Earth by God's choice. Therefore, in order to bring His Kingdom on Earth to rid the world of the curse of the tree of knowledge of good and evil, He had to send forth His Word in the flesh.

Jesus was the Son of Man and the Son of God. His mother was Mary which made him the son of man. But the Holy Spirit planted His seed in Mary which made Jesus the Son of God. Jesus then had both physical and spiritual authority. While Jesus was in heaven as **The Word of God**, he had spiritual authority but could only work through humans. God had given us the physical authority. So, Jesus had to become both the son of Man and the Son of God in order to be our Tree of Life.

Where we get confused is the Gospels are the beginning of God's Kingdom on earth. We keep wanting to go back to Jesus' words in the gospels and, then, we stay stagnant. This is especially true when it comes to healing. We read the accounts of the individual healings, tear them down, and make teachings from them. Meanwhile, Jesus was always pointing the disciples past the cross. Yet, we derive "hidden meanings" from the miracles that Jesus performed, which is exactly what is holding us back.

> *Verily, verily, I say unto you, He that believeth on me, the works that I do shall he do also; and greater works than these shall he do; because I go unto My Father. (John 14:12)*

Jesus was pointing past his resurrection. Yet, we want to stop and see what lessons we are to learn from Jesus asking the demons their names. Time to move forward away from bad teachings. What happens is confusion when we try to place things that have already happened for a specific purpose directly into our time.

> *So, likewise ye, when ye see these things come to*

> *pass, know ye that the kingdom of God is nigh at hand. Verily I say unto you, this generation shall not pass away till all be fulfilled. Heaven and earth shall pass away: but my words shall not pass away. (Luke 21:31-33)*

The majority of the time, He referred to himself as the son man. Healing had been done before through the Levitical Priesthood. That isn't what captured the attention of the people or the Pharisees. What captured their attention were the specific miracles that Jesus performed. These are the very miracles we break down and make theories about healing around. Instead, they were miracles for a specific purpose: to prove that Jesus was the Messiah. These were miracles that had never been performed before. Only the son of God could perform these miracles.

Each one of these miracles, involved sin according to the Jewish Mindset. Also, most of these were performed on the Sabbath Day. The miracles that only the Messiah could perform were part of the unwritten law, but now are written in the Talmud. The supporting scriptures that are in our bibles are found in Isaiah. The four miracles were healing leprosy, those born with defects, deaf-mute spirits, and raising the dead after three days.

> *To open the blind eyes, to bring out the prisoners from the prison, and them that sit in darkness out of the prison house. (Isaiah 42:7)*

> *Then the eyes of the blind shall be opened, and the ears of the deaf shall be unstopped. Then shall the lame man leap as an hart, and the tongue of the dumb sing: for in the wilderness shall water break out, and streams in the desert. (Isaiah 35:5-6)*

Leprosy. This was viewed as direct punishment from God. Only Moses, Miriam and Naaman, had been healed from it, all of these prior to the Law of Moses. No Jew born under the Law of Moses had ever been healed from leprosy. God through Moses had set up specific guidelines to be followed to prove that the leper was cleansed. This was never used until Jesus.

Deaf Mute Spirit. The priests were able to cast out demons, but there were guidelines to be followed. They had to ask the demon its name and cast it out by the name. The priests were unable to cast out these spirits because they could not respond.

The man from the tombs of Gadarenes is one case of the deaf mute spirit being cast out by Jesus. The reason He asks the name of this demon, is not to adhere to this code, but to prove that He was the son of God. This demon wouldn't respond to anyone except the Son of God. This was the only time that Jesus asks the name of a demon. Yet, how many theologies has man made of this one incident?

Birth defects. No person had ever been healed from birth defects. It was based off of Exodus 34:6-7, visiting the iniquity of fathers to the third and fourth generation. The specific defects healed by Jesus were lame from birth and born blind. Please note, God rescinded this in the whole chapter of Ezekiel more specifically in 18:*20:*

> *The soul that sinneth, it shall die. The son shall not bear the iniquity of the father, neither shall the father bear the iniquity of the son:...*

Raised from the dead after 72 hours. Once the body had decayed, it was believed that only the Son of God could raise it. Lazarus is our example of this fulfillment. How many theologies have been made that healing is God's timing? It is based on Jesus putting off going to Lazarus. It was a onetime event to prove that Jesus was the Messiah, the Son of God.

First of all, pay special attention to this. Up until chapter ten in Matthew, Jesus hadn't commanded His disciples to heal the sick. He was first fulfilling the four miracles. He was also being first observed by the religious leaders, then questioned, and then judged.

The first few miracles of these types, Jesus commands the person not to say anything to anyone but to go to the priests. The reason was as a testimony. The first time was with the leper. They went through the process of determining if the leper had been cleansed. This was the very first time that rite had been enacted. Now, Jesus was on the radar. The Pharisees and Sadducee's then were sent out to observe Jesus. They just observed at first. As these miracles continued, they went into the questioning phase. The best example of this is the man born blind. The whole chapter nine of John is about this miracle, how the leadership is questioning the man's parents to determine if he were truly born blind, then, if he were truly healed. Finally, the man is questioned. His answer was directly from heaven:

> *Since the world began was it not heard that any man opened the eyes of one that was born blind. If this man were not of God he could do nothing. (John 9:32-33, KJV)*

The final judgement of the Pharisees comes when they declared that Jesus cast out devils by the devil. Then Jesus makes His judgment as well:

> *But when the Pharisees heard it, they said, this fellow doth, not cast out devils, but by Beelzebub the prince of the devils....*
> *Wherefore I say unto you, All manner of sin and blasphemy shall be forgiven unto men: but the blasphemy against the Holy Ghost shall not be forgiven unto men. (Matthew 12:24,31)*

The reason that Jesus states this is because, just like Annias and Sapphira in the Book of Acts, the Pharisees had lied and blasphemed directly against the Holy Spirit. These were acts that could only be performed through the Son of God. They were totally preordained miracles set for that time period. Once performed by Jesus, then all believers could do the same. It is after He performs them that He sends the disciples forth to heal the sick, cleanse the lepers, and raise the dead.

Are you starting to see that the individual healings set forth in the gospels aren't there to show us how to heal the sick? They were there for a specific purpose. Take away those individual healings and all that's left are those who have faith for their healing. Our lessons in healing come after the Cross, after the day of Pentecost, when those who believe became sons of God.

John the Baptist when imprisoned didn't send forth his disciples because his faith was waning. Nope. Not one bit. It was out of faith. He knew of these miracles. Jesus' response shows us the Truth.

> *Jesus answered and said unto them, Go and shew John again those things which ye do hear and see. The blind receive their sight, and the lame walk, the lepers are cleansed, and the deaf hear, the dead are raised up, and the poor have the gospel preached to them. And blessed is he, whosoever shall not be offended in me. (Matthew 11:4-6)*

All of these miracles have three things in common, all the people marvel. Jesus declares that these works were for the Son of God to be glorified, or words to that effect. We get wrong theologies from them.

> *When Jesus heard that, he said, This sickness is not unto death, but for the glory of God, that the Son of God might be glorified thereby. (John 11:4)*

> *Therefore, the Jews sought the more to kill him, because he not only had broken the sabbath, but said also that God was his Father, making himself equal with God. (John 5:18)*

> *...See thou tell no man, but go thy way shew thyself to the priest, and offer the gift that Moses commanded, for a testimony unto them. (Matthew 8:4b)*

> *Jesus heard that they had cast him out; and when he had found him, he said unto him, Dost thou believe on the Son of God? (John 9:35)*
>
> *And cried with a loud voice, and said, What have I to do with thee, Jesus, thou Son of the most high God? (Mark 5:7b)*

Understand why these miracles were performed. Then, understanding of healing is perfected. There were only two types of miraculous individual accounts of healing performed, those who already had the faith to be healed and those that were of the four miracles that only the Christ could perform. Scratch the latter miracles out of the picture and every wrong belief about healing is removed.

The most detrimental belief is that a person can be healed against their own unbelief. This is detrimental because a person that isn't healed then seeks out another person to heal them. They get prayed for by numbers of people thinking of finding that one person that has the "power" to break through their unbelief. Then, God is blamed, the other person is blamed, the one who isn't healed feels condemned. There is no winning in this situation.

Yet, the person does not know what part of them is in unbelief. They are confused, condemned, and give up. In most cases, this person has seen numbers of people healed themselves. They do believe in healing and have seen it.

I want to restate it again and again so I'm not taken the wrong way: **We absolutely should pray for the sick.** There is hope for everyone. But first, I have to completely destroy the concept that Tony or others, can "punch through" unbelief for you. If you don't believe you're healed, then you can't recognize that you are. As a man believes, so is he. You absolutely can be healed. So, keep reading and bear with me.

Take away the four miracles that only the Messiah could perform.

Granted, many of these people were in unbelief, because they couldn't be healed until Jesus. Present day, everyone can be healed. But set those healings aside. All that's left are those who had faith for their healing. Here are the examples:

> *Then Jesus answered and said unto her, O woman, great is thy faith: be it unto thee even as thou wilt.... (Matthew 15:28)*
>
> *Then touched he their eyes, saying, According to your faith be it unto you. (Matthew 9:29)*
>
> *But Jesus turned him about, and when he saw her, he said Daughter, be of good comfort; thy faith hath made thee whole.... (Matthew 9:22)*
>
> *And Jesus answered and said unto him. What wilt thou that I should do unto thee? The blind man said unto him, Lord, that I might receive my sight. And Jesus said unto him, Go thy way: thy faith hath made thee whole... (Mark 10:51-52)*
>
> *But when he saw the wind boisterous, he was afraid: and beginning to sink, he cried, saying Lord, save me. And immediately Jesus stretched, forth his hand, and caught him, and said unto him, O thou of little faith, wherefore didst thou doubt. (Matthew 14:30-31)*

Jesus, standing right in front of Peter with faith, could not keep Peter from sinking. Jesus had to physically pull him up to safety. Once you take the four miracles that only the Messiah could perform and set them aside, Jesus attributes the healing to the person's faith. Good news post cross: You do have the faith, the Holy Spirit, who is the spirit of faith.

When Jesus is resurrected, everything changed. He is completely transformed. Now, He has been given all power both on the Earth and in the heavens. He commands the disciples to go into all the nations.

> *And Jesus came and spake unto them, saying, All power is given unto me in heaven and in earth. (Matthew 28:18)*

We truly do not get the scope of this! Everything has changed, yet Christianity has remained stale because we haven't moved past the gospels. Jesus is the foundation. What good is a foundation if there's nothing built upon it? Christ taught the Kingdom of God. That isn't the pinnacle. The pinnacle is Paul's Gospel of Christ, within whom we are now one. As of the Day of Pentecost, we are one spirit with the Lord who is giving life to your mortal body.

7 NO LONGER MERE MORTALS

Jesus is the completed integration of mankind. He is now fully complete. He is now higher than the angels. He is a representation of what we are in the process of becoming. Indeed, we've actually had access to being more like Jesus now than we could ever imagine.

First, we must learn that God's Kingdom is fully on the Earth. Secondly, we have the Holy Spirit within us, that must become real. We must stop separating the spiritual from the physical world. Right now, we are like Adam and Eve before the fall except better, because now, we're exactly as Christ is. Coffee break time!

Do you know that the tree of Life is no longer in the Garden of Eden? The tree of Life is inside of you! His Name is Christ Jesus and it is His Spirit that resides within you. We don't have to look outside of ourselves for healing or anything else that most would consider supernatural. You are a branch that is being fed from the tree of life that is within. The more we grasp that concept, the less we rely on our physical senses.

Our physical senses are taking information from the outside world which is keeping us bound to the limits of the physical nature of things. There is a greater truth and it is running from inside of us to the outside world. Paul and the other early Believers had the first fruits of the Spirit. Yet, they were waiting for events to transpire for the fullest revelation.

> *And not only they, but ourselves also, which have the firstfruits of the Spirit, even we ourselves groan within ourselves, waiting for the adoption, to wit, the redemption of our body. (Romans 8:23)*

The Apostles had the first fruits of the Spirit. The revelations of Paul were for his time period and part of foundational Christianity, but not in its completeness. That will be a hard swallow for many of you and I do not intend to go into the complexities of it. Through Paul and the other Apostles, we get a glimpse of what we should be looking like today, but it's just a glimpse: Paul and his cloths, Peter and his shadow, Paul and the poisonous snake…. And not only these things, also everything Paul underwent: the stoning, the whippings, the shipwrecks, being beaten with rods… All of these things he survived supernaturally. Neither Paul nor the other disciples ever struggled from disease and neither should we.

The problem is the way we look at it. The modern-day church thinks that one certain person has to pray over believers. That's not true. This comes from James, who was writing to Jews. They were used to the temple system and having to go to the priesthood. Once again, we don't look at the context or who the writer is talking to. All Believers are priests. We can be healed on our own.

> *And hath made us kings and priests unto God and his Father; to him be glory and dominion for ever and ever. Amen. (Revelation 1:6)*

There are two distinctions to make: is the person a believer or unbeliever? With an unbeliever there is a transfer of the Holy Spirit, they don't have the Holy Spirit, so you are imparting Him to them. With believers we already have the Holy Spirit there is no impartation needed, and we are all priests unto The Father. A believer praying for another believer isn't giving them anything they don't already have. There is no transfer of power and the way ministers have it appear is that they have a "power" another believer doesn't have. This is wrong. So, quit thinking that you're Harry Potter performing magic! You're not.

This is also why many believers don't get healed. They think that they have to look outside the Holy Spirit who is in them. They are trying to get something that they feel is missing in themselves. You may ask, then, about the sensations people often feel. These sensations are coming from the Holy Spirit within them to increase their eager anticipation or confident expectation.

The scenario that is happening is this. When I speak life to another believer, or say, "Be healed," it is my expectation that is causing the person to believe that something happened. That person can now recognize or acknowledge they are healed. They were actually healed long before I came along. They were just unable to recognize this until they became expectant. It was my confident expectation based on my belief that Holy Spirit was already giving life to their mortal body, that they were already healed. They can now recognize improvement and acknowledge that they are healed. This has nothing to do with a transfer of "Power" or my breaking through their unbelief.

Healing was already attained for us, what Jesus accomplished was us receiving Holy Spirit and becoming sons of God. We aren't trying to pull our healing from the spiritual world into the physical world. Healing isn't coming from the heavens into our body. It's already within our body in the form of Holy Spirit.

Why does your body live in the first place? Because your spirit is inside of your body. When we accept that God has raised Jesus from the dead, His Holy Spirit joins with our spirit and we become one spirit with the Lord. We need only to recognize that there is improvement and then we'll be able to acknowledge that we are healed.

> *And if Christ be in you, the body is dead because of sin; but the Spirit is life because of righteousness. But if the Spirit of him that raised up Jesus from the dead dwell in you, he that raised up Christ from the dead shall also quicken your mortal bodies by his Spirit that dwelleth in you. (Romans 8:10-11)*

In other words, Holy Spirit is giving life to your body, an always happening event when we believe it. Do you now understand what is going on when one believer prays for another? A person states they don't believe in healing, you then pray for them. Because of your expectation, they can recognize change and acknowledge they are healed. This is not you imparting power, rather it is your expectation being contagious, so now they can feel the improvement and acknowledge they are healed. The veil is now ripped from their face and they can see the healing. It is the same when you see your own healing. It's just easier to do with another person because you aren't feeling the symptoms!

The wrong perception is what keeps people from recognizing their healing. This goes hand in hand with the wrong belief that there is one anointed person that can break through another person's will, the dramatic scenario, the way churches display healing, and our perception of the gospels. We think there has to be a dramatic display, what I call fireworks. We're looking for all the emotional stuff and the feeling that God Almighty is coming down from heaven to touch you personally.

Pay attention. He's already inside of you and He's been guiding you, to your healing, since the day you became sick. If you believe you're healed, then you are. There doesn't have to be the dramatic scene that churches and media display. In most cases, the person healed does not experience healing the way it is imagined. Indeed, my original healing was dramatic, and I felt the liquid gold peace.

The rest of my healings, there wasn't all of that. Many people miss out on acknowledging their healing because they think they should be experiencing emotional fireworks. If it doesn't happen the way they perceive it to be, then in their minds they aren't healed.

A miracle healing is oftentimes what that person makes it out to be. Healing is always available. We just have to recognize improvement and acknowledge that we're healed. Don't miss out on your healing by the perception of what it should look or feel like. Many times, the symptoms melt away long before the person even recognizes that they are gone.

Many people will have a miracle and never recognize it. Often, people will tell me that they've never seen a miracle. During the course of our conversation, they will bring up a condition that they used to have. Suddenly, they realize that one day it just went away. That would be a miracle. This is huge!

We must become sensitive to miracles. The more you can recognize a miracle, then the more miracles you'll see because you become expectant for them. We think all miracles come with the fireworks: No fireworks, no miracle. Nope. That's wrong thinking.

Take a moment sit back, take a sip of coffee, and think about a time where you had a symptom that suddenly vanished. Ask Holy Spirit to bring it to your remembrance. I'll give you a minute. Here's a testimony in the meantime.

I was praying for a woman over the phone when I had a word of knowledge. I stated, "Your right elbow will get locked up and often there will be a sharp pain." At first, she said no. Then she thought about it. She gets excited and says, "Yes! My elbow used to be messed up. It's been fine for years." She then recognized that it had been a miracle. The whole reason Holy Spirit showed me this was so she would recognize that miracle and be expectant for a miracle with her current health condition. She was then able to acknowledge her healing with the current problem.

How many miracles like this have you experienced? Probably at least three or four. Write them down, get excited about them, and recognize miracles happen every day. We either rationalize them away or don't think about them in that way. Recognizing the miracles of the past will help you to acknowledge your present miracle. In fact, I'll boldly state that the more sensitive to miracles you become, the more you'll walk in divine health. Then, health issues will become a thing of the past. Honestly, I would never lie to you.

Healing is not magic, nor does it have to be a dramatic display, but it is a common occurrence. It's not just a once in lifetime, supernatural event, but as a natural, ever happening, daily part of a believer's life. We have been reborn, so we have a new father, new DNA, new life. We are no longer subject to the laws that the natural world would think of as normal. My Father who resides in me is the creator of the universe. I am now reborn into being the very fabric of His Essence. My Father is an immortal being as am I. Therefore, that which others consider as supernatural, I consider with great gratitude to be normal. The more you think about this, the more sensitive to acknowledging these truths you will become, the more you'll see.

Fill a glass jar full of lady bugs and make sure you punch some holes in it. That way, they won't die on you. Stare at them continually for, say, ten hours (I'm joking, kind of). After that time, walk outside. The only bugs you'll see will be lady bugs. You'll spot them right away. You won't recognize any other types of bugs. Your eyes will immediately pick out the lady bugs. You'll spot lady bugs coming from a distance. The same is true of the "supernatural" things of Our Father. The more you focus on it, the easier it'll naturally occur, and the easier acknowledging those instances will be. Paul states to focus on the things above, not the things of this Earth. In heaven, divine health is natural not supernatural. There is no disease. Therefore, the same is true on Earth now.

Here's an example from my life. I've been bald since the young age of thirty-five. Suddenly I noticed hair growing where it hasn't grown in some twenty years. My hair stylist recognized it without me even pointing it out. When our revelation grows of who we are, then the miraculous just naturally starts happening, not because I'm so holy, but because of who's inside of me. I should add that I haven't made any declarations or prayers for hair. Being bald never bothered me. The resulting hair growth is because of my sensitivity to the things of My father.

Another example of miracles just happening is that I had cracked the face plate glass on my smart phone. I threw the phone on my desk and walked away from it. I returned to it after about an hour later. The phone was completely whole. I am digressing a bit, and probably opening up pandora's box as well.

My main point is, the more we acknowledge the miraculous things of the Holy spirit, the more grateful we are, and the more often they will happen. Recognizing miraculous healings is just a starting point to leading a divinely healthy life.

8 MERCY AND RIGHTEOUSNESS

Blessed be the God and Father of our Lord Jesus Christ, which according to his abundant mercy hath begotten us again unto a lively hope by the resurrection of Jesus Christ from the dead, to an inheritance incorruptible, and undefiled, and that fadeth not away, reserved in heaven for you.
(1 Peter 1:3-4)

...which in time past were not a people, but are now the people of God: which had not obtained mercy, but now have obtained mercy. (1 Peter 2:10)

Coffee time! Take a five-minute break while you contemplate the mercy of God.

We often think that God's mercy is needed every day. There is a much deeper meaning. When it comes to healing, adapt this line of thought. It was by The Father's mercy that we have the Everlasting New Covenant. He poured out His Mercy by sending us His Son so that now, we are sons of God. That is the ultimate mercy of God, He sent us Jesus. All of mankind has received eternal mercy for those that are In Christ. It is by His Mercy that now we have the righteousness of God through faith in the Son. It is through this one-time act of mercy that we obtain righteousness, therefore divine health and healing. It is by this one act of mercy, that is not able to be withdrawn, that we know confidently that we are already healed now. Jesus now sits on the throne of David establishing our righteousness.

> *And in mercy shall the throne be established: and he shall sit upon it in truth in the tabernacle of David, judging, and seeking judgment, and hasting righteousness. (Isaiah 16:5)*

I want you to really understand this. The mercy of God was that, by sending us Christ, His blood Covenant with the Father cannot be withdrawn. Therefore, it is by that one act that we are guaranteed to be healed. Our healing does not have anything to do with our actions because we received the ultimate show of mercy. This mercy is everlasting. Therefore, when I expect to be healed I will be. There is even a greater Truth coming up. But first, be convinced that we have received eternal mercy. Through this one-time act, the world of darkness cannot force sickness upon us, neither can our actions prevent a healing. The problem is we keep wanting to believe that sickness comes upon us because of our actions. Then, we have to beg for mercy that the Father already granted us.

So, do what it takes to get it through to your mind and heart. As long as we are believers that believe that God has raised Jesus from the dead, we have an eternal mercy. Many will argue this point with me. But the next step that goes hand in hand with this eternal mercy should shut you up, to be blunt.

Oops! Sorry for getting a little harsh there, but it was needed. **When we recognize this, we should be eternally grateful therefore we do not sin willfully.** We have the mind of Christ. Therefore, when we focus on the things of the Spirit, we will not sin. The eternal mercy we've been given, therefore, leads us smack into another gift that is freely given.

> *For therein is the righteousness of God revealed from faith to faith: as it is written the just shall live by faith. (Romans 1:17)*

I have to interject. It is from faith to faith: From faith in the Law of

Moses to Faith in God. This is two faiths, not from faith, to faith, to faith, to faith (as many preachers teach). Rather, from faith in works to the faith In Christ. Just wanted to get that settled from the get-go. Let's continue:

> *Even the righteousness of God which is by faith of Jesus Christ unto all and upon all them that believe for there is no difference. (Romans 3:22)*

That free gift is the righteousness of God through the faith of Christ Jesus. I am now righteous. Therefore, nothing of evil can touch me when I really believe that I am the righteousness of God. This has no basis whatsoever upon my actions. We are going to build upon that in a minute. The righteousness of God is what makes us sons of God and gives us all the inheritances of Christ. Included among that is divine health and healing.

> *Herein is our love made perfect, that we may have boldness in the day of judgment: because as he is, so are we in this world. (1 John 4:17)*

I know you're starting to rationalize this, so just stop it already. You're thinking, well, if I eat junk food, then I set myself up for poor health. If I do this, then I deserve that. Which is exactly why I walked you through the history of mankind with the first six chapters. That is what human wisdom has taught you. That's thinking through the mind of the first Adam, not being transformed by the renewing of the mind to the mind of Christ. Through Jesus, we are now righteous which means we are now a temple of the Holy Spirit just as Jesus was thereby making us sons of God.

The more revelation that you attain that we are righteous through faith in Jesus, the more inherently eternal life is manifested in our bodies, on which all the gifts of God are based. Can you imagine Jesus being in his earthly ministry sick? Can you imagine Jesus in His glorified body being sick? Can you imagine Holy Spirit within you being sick? **I am not instructing you to eat unhealthily**. I always need to use that disclaimer. Come to terms with this: that you are the righteousness of God. Therefore, nothing in its physical state can affect you when you are walking in the Spirit focused on the spiritual nature of things.

This takes a true renewing of the mind and none of us are there completely. But the more we understand this, the more we'll walk in it. Challenge everything! Think about how Jesus was when He walked on the Earth. He could touch anything without fear, this can and should be the way Believers walk. The more you come to realize that we have received God's Mercy by Him sending Jesus and that through Jesus we are completely righteous, the more mature believers we'll become. **Disclaimer: We are meant to interact with this world. So, don't be stupid! Don't try to drive a car with your eyes closed or the many other stupid actions one could think of.**

> *But ye are not in the flesh but in the Spirit, if so be that the Spirit of God dwell in you. Now if any man have not the Spirit of Christ, he is none of his. And if Christ be in you, the body is dead because of sin, but the Spirit is life because of righteousness. But if the Spirit of him that raised up Jesus from the dead dwell in you, he that raised up Christ from the dead shall also quicken your mortal bodies by his Spirit that dwelleth in you. (Romans 8:9-11)*

Now to paraphrase this because of the righteousness of Christ, we have his Holy Spirit who is giving life to our mortal bodies. This is one of my favorite verses. This is the biggest reason that the miraculous just seems to happen around me. I'm going to share it with you. I always see The Spirit of Christ active within me, now it is almost automatic so that no matter what I'm doing, He is active, giving life to my mortal body, and therefore, always flowing through me. Since He is always within me active, I'm always protected and lots of miracles occur without me saying a word. Here's just a few examples then I'll walk you through how I got to this point.

Two days ago, I was eating at a restaurant and the waitress was serving my drink. My phone was sitting right beside where she was setting the drink. She knocked the drink over. It should've gotten all over me and the phone. Yet, there wasn't so much as a drop on either me or the phone. The waitress was amazed and kept saying that was impossible. I then got to be a witness to her:

> I hit myself with the sledgehammer, no pain, no swelling, I didn't even speak a word. Then, I got right back to work.

> Many times me and semi-trucks shared the same space. I should've been smashed against the mountain side. No damage came to me or my car.

> Cars have pulled out right in front of me, should've been no way of avoiding it. Yet, I end up on the other side of the car with no damage.

> A man shot at me point blank range. The bullet went through the windshield, didn't go through me.

The way it all started was around a year after my healing during my quiet time with the Lord. I would lay on the floor pondering specific scripture. These are paraphrased: The shield of faith is quenching all the fiery darts of the wicked. Holy Spirit in me is giving life to my body. Me and the Lord are one spirit, so nothing can harm me. I would think about these verses. Then, one day I imagined fire like the way I would imagine the burning bush inside of my chest.

The first time this image just came across my thoughts. After that, I would purposefully imagine it. At first, it was small inside my chest. But as time wore on, it became bigger. I got to the point that, while I was working, I would think about these verses and imagine the fire superimposed on my body. During times where miracles would be needed, I would think about one of those verses and just see the image of Holy Spirit superimposed on me in the image of my person. After a few years, the image turned into water and I would recall one of those verses. This made Holy Spirit personal to me.

Many believers lack the knowing that He is always with us and active. This is in keeping with scriptures as Holy Spirit is described as fire, water, oil, and a dove. So, while I would go about my day, I would think, "I am one spirit with the Lord. So, He is giving life to my body," or one of the other scriptures. It makes Holy Spirit a real person and not just a "force" or someone out there in heaven. This also makes scripture real and not just a cute little saying.

The last two years or so, this is more or less automatic. "Out of the belly come rivers of flowing water," was another one I frequently used. I would imagine Holy Spirit as water flowing from my spirit, to my soul, then body, then like a river rushing outward to the world. If Holy Spirit is flowing outward, then the world can't get in. Also, the Holy Spirit as a river of water is cleansing my body washing all impurities outward. Think of it like this. If you have a garden hose that is turned off insects can get in. But if it's turned on nothing can get in. Being one spirit with the Lord, if He is active and flowing outward, nothing from the outside world can get in.

The thing to understand is that we have to have an active relationship with Holy Spirit. This is just what has worked for me. Reciting scriptures verbatim is not personal. So often, we think the power of scriptures is in the written word. There is no power coming from written words, many people have recited scriptures for years and still die. The power of the Holy Spirit flows when we believe what we're speaking from the heart. Change scripture into your own speech the way you talk. Make them meaningful. I often relate this to a letter.

If I write a letter to one person, then simply change the name on the letter and send it to someone else, that letter would make no sense to them. This is the same with scripture.

The scriptures were not written by me, nor were they even written in English. I don't speak Aramaic or Greek. So, the words coming out of my mouth aren't even the same words as were originally written by the author.

You are one spirit with the Lord Jesus. So, He conforms to your personality. He communicates with you in ways only you can understand. So, forget the of the strict standards of a religious mindset and make your relationship with The Father, Son, and Holy Spirit an individual relationship.

9 RECOGNIZING, NOT RECEIVING

That last chapter was a good one. Are you healed yet? Did some light bulbs turn on? Let's have us some freshly roasted Cadejo coffee while you look for the improvement that is there. Please consider that I knew none of this stuff prior to my healing. Then again, I didn't have a lifetime of wrong religious beliefs in my system. This section may start out as if I'm splitting hairs with my words. I'm not. I'm splitting logs. Perspective is everything.

The formula is always the same: we take it as an unquestionable fact that we're healed (believe), we expect improvement, then we receive. Scratch that out. Let me explain.

Many people have a problem with saying, "I believe I am healed." Holy Spirit is within me giving life to my body so there has to be improvement. That is how you can look at it. Looking at it that way, you can say I am healed, and stay focused on looking to recognize improvement. Right above I used the words 'then we receive our healing.' Nearly everyone that teaches healing uses the word receive. Change the way you think on that. I'm not looking to receive my healing because I'm already healed. I'm looking to recognize improvement so that I can acknowledge my healing.

The words we use to explain things shows where our thoughts lie. The meaning of the word receive is misleading. Receive means to grab or to take possession of, and it implies we are taking possession of something we ain't got. When it comes to healing, when we think receive my healing, now I'm implying that I'm looking outside of my body for my healing. Holy Spirit is inside of me giving life to my body, therefore I have my healing. Quit looking to the outside world for something you already have.

From the abundance of the heart the mouth speaks. If then I say that you need to receive your healing, then I'm agreeing with you that you don't have your healing. My paraphrase of Jesus words is, if we believe we have received, then we shall have it. We must than believe that we have already received our healing to have it. Saying or thinking that you must receive your healing, becomes a declaration that we aren't healed. That turns into a huge search on how to grab your healing and take it into yourself. Then, we have to look for reasons why we aren't receiving our healing which is how all the wrong methods come about.

A method is a process to attain an object. Once again, we're implying we don't have our healing. That is the very foundation of unbelief. The method is the Cross, by which we have the righteousness of God, and through whom we receive Holy Spirit, who is always giving life to our body. The methods are not inner healing, courtrooms of heavens, eating right or the many other methods taught.

I cannot stress this enough! If we are searching to receive, then that is stating that we don't have our healing. **That is Unbelief!** Please tell me the light bulb went off. Yes, people do get healed by those methods because at some point they come to believe they have received. They are then reliant on that method, which sometimes works. Most of the time, it doesn't. Then, because the basis of their belief wasn't the Cross and Holy Spirit, when something else happens, they are right back to the drawing board.

On the other hand, when I know I'm already healed, then I expect to recognize improvement. Next, I can acknowledge that I am truly healed. Instead of trying to receive, I'm simply recognizing the improvement. Then, it is a simpler matter of seek and you shall find, knock and the door is open. I'm no longer trying to go outside of Holy Spirit who is in my spirit to find something I ain't got. Once this is clearly set in your mind, that now you simply have to recognize improvement, then suddenly the symptoms melt away.

Have you seen one of those pixilated pictures where there are images hidden inside? At first glance you don't see any images, then you stare at it for a period of time an image starts to form. Then you can recognize the image. The image was there all along you simply didn't recognize it.

The clouds outside: you're in a rush and you look up at the clouds in the sky. If you're rushing around, it's likely that there are no images. Yet, if you're not rushed and stare at the clouds looking for an image in a concentrated effort, then an image suddenly forms. Unless you're an artistic person, artistic people spot images pretty quickly. This is exactly how healing is.

We were healed by Jesus wounds, bruises, and His blood being poured out. The healing already exists within our body because of His sacrifice. Holy Spirit within us is always giving life to our mortal body. We just have to recognize it. Just like with the cloud formations, if we aren't focused on finding an image within the clouds, we won't see the images. The clouds will then just stay little wisps twirling around in the air. These simple perception changes make a huge difference. Now, I'm looking for the improvement, not for the symptom, and I'm looking simply to recognize what's already there.

Hidden object games are another excellent example as well. There are objects hidden within the picture that must be found. There are specific objects to find. At first glance, it is difficult to spot the specific objects. You know they are there, so you keep looking for them. You keep searching because there is no doubt in your mind that the objects are there. That's the difference between trying to receive something or simply recognizing improvement. If you're looking knowing that improvement is there, then you will find it and be able to acknowledge your healing. If on the other hand the perception is on receiving, then from the start, you question that it's there.

With the hidden object game, if you can't find the object, would you tell yourself I lack faith? Or I haven't received the right picture? Or the image doesn't exist within the picture? Would you think to say well maybe because I sinned, the image disappeared? We could go insane and say things like that, but most of us wouldn't. Some people like myself will only look so long, give up, and walk away. Other people would use help methods within the game. Then suddenly, we see the images and we kick ourselves. They were there all along!

Did a light bulb go off? We always have our healing, we have to know that without questioning. Then just like with the hidden object game, we just have to recognize where the image is. We can come up with lame reasons why we aren't recognizing our healing or we can acknowledge that it is there and eagerly anticipate improvement. We keep to the formula we believe, expect to recognize improvement, then we can acknowledge our healing.

We are already healed, that is an unquestionable fact. Set it down in concrete. It is always available because Holy Spirit is giving life to our body. If we are hit or miss, then we give up and walk away. Just like people would do with a hidden object game. When we know that we are already healed, then we confidently expect or eagerly anticipate improvement. Then, before our very eyes, the symptoms just melt away. This is like a veil suddenly being ripped off of our face. Then, we are suddenly healthy.

Back to the hidden object game, when you're looking to recognize a particular object, you will find that object. Same with healing. Whatever your looking for is what you'll find. Either symptoms or improvement. Sometimes, while playing the hidden object game, you can't recognize the object. Your spouse then walks up and finds the object for you. My wife loves hidden object games. It helps her when I walk up behind her and immediately spot the object she's been looking for. There she was for five minutes or so looking for one certain object, and I walk up and say, "There it is."

When we pray for others, that is what is happening. I am spotting the improvement for them. Now, they can recognize their improvement and acknowledge that they are healed. They already have their healing, I am simply enabling them to acknowledge it for themselves. I am not experiencing their symptoms, so it is obviously easier for me to recognize it for them. That is what praying for others is all about. Just like my finding my wife's hidden object, I had fresh eyes. So, in two seconds, I could recognize what she'd been missing for five minutes.

Do you understand? Recognizing and acknowledging our healing is a matter of perception. What are we looking for? We are either looking for how to receive or recognizing that we have received. Common sense should dictate which way is more effective? Please, change how you perceive healing. Your words will change, and then, divine health is two seconds away.

Before we go much farther, one question I'm asked is what about people that are unconscious or the dead? You can't explain this to them. What about unbelievers?

When I walk up to them, I am believing that they are already healed. Then, I'm recognizing improvement for them. They wake up and are able to acknowledge that they are healed.

Remember, I myself was healed without this knowledge. The difference is these types of people most likely haven't even sought to be healed. They aren't faced with all the contradictions that those who already believe in healing have been taught, therefore, there's less resistance. Also, I am using the physical words to show the spiritual which is what Jesus did through parables. The things I'm describing are what is going on under the surface that enables the miracle to be recognized.

We look at the individual accounts of healing with Jesus, then think He healed people in different ways. That is the surface level. The truth is it was the same way every time. The person had to believe, then recognize the improvement, then acknowledge their healing. That time period was different. The Holy Spirit hadn't been poured out on all flesh. They had to go to the priests, disciples, or Jesus. The majority had faith that Jesus would heal them. There were the crowds that were healed!

If they were here in the present day, they wouldn't have needed anyone to pray for them. In fact, I would go so far to say those people would have never gotten sick in the first place. The Holy Spirit has been poured out and is inside of the Believer. He is giving life to your body. We are now the priesthood. So, you can be healed right where you're at, right this moment. We no longer have to look outside of ourselves for healing.

Let's go back to the hidden object game for a second. I'm looking for an object. It's been 30 minutes and it can't be found. The thought crosses my mind that the designer made an error and left the object out. What will happen? I'll decide that the designer left the object out and give up. Perhaps I'll get another hidden object game. That thought of designer error has already been planted in me. I look for 20 minutes for an object and can't find it. Since, in my prior experience a seed has been planted, I give up earlier than before. I get a different hidden object game. This time, after ten minutes of looking, I can't find the object. Now, I'm thinking all designers are messing up. I quit playing hidden object games all together.

Unknown to me, in the original game I'd been looking for the wrong object all along. I had misread what object I'd been looking for. That caused a lie to be implanted in my head, got me frustrated, and therefore, I gave up the game altogether.

This is exactly what happens with healing. We keep looking at it the wrong way. Frustration sets in and we give up. Then, we come up with all sorts of reasons why we didn't get healed. This leads to rabbit trail, after rabbit trail.

We first must believe that we are healed already. We discussed how to believe that. Holy Spirit is giving life to my body, so I can now believe that I'm healed. The next rabbit trail we discussed was the difference between recognizing what has to be there, or trying to receive what we think we ain't got. We can either look to recognize the improvement or the symptom. The wrong object to look for would be the symptom. Yet, we do that automatically because we use the wrong template as the determining factor.

The template we use is our body instead of Holy Spirit inside of us. This is the difference. We use our physical senses to determine for us whether we are healed or not. The body then becomes the template or the gauge for our healing.

The control center for the physical senses is the brain. It is filling in the blanks. This is automatic. It's on auto pilot and doesn't know the things of God.

Right now, I'm touching my dog, Ariel. That is the truth. I can rely on my physical senses for that. Our bodies are given to us for interacting with the physical world.

I can trust my physical senses when it comes to driving my car. I see a green light turn to yellow, then red. I had better trust that by stepping on the brakes, the car will stop. I see a car turn right in front of me. I'd better trust that and swerve or do what I need to do in order to avoid contact.

Another example, I'm hugging my wife. That is the truth. This is interaction with the physical world.

However, when it comes to sicknesses, diseases, and injuries, the physical senses do not understand that Jesus gave His body for ours. The brain doesn't comprehend this, nor can it. The brain is a piece of equipment. We can't rely on it to tell us we're healed. In fact, it is the brain releasing the symptoms. Pain for instance is the brain releasing the signals for pain. Therefore, I can't use my body as the blueprint of whether I'm healed or not. This is the same as questioning whether the designer of the hidden object game put the object within the game. We might as well give it up and not start the game.

I'm already healed because Holy Spirit is giving life to my body. That is the Truth. My body letting me feel pain is a lie. The very thinking that I can get sick is a lie. I'm walking along and I feel a stabbing pain. I recognize the pain as a lie. The truth is I am healed. That has to be my reaction. Be convinced that a lie is a lie and the truth is the truth. My mindset is always that Holy Spirit is giving life to my body. Therefore, I'm always healed. Since I am healed, there has to be improvement.

The flip side of that is, if my body is the gauge and decider of whether I'm healed or not, then I am looking to see if the pain is still there. In my mind, if there is pain, then I'm not healed. That is huge! Am I looking **to see if the pain is still there or looking knowing there has to be improvement.** The question then comes along, what happens if I can't recognize improvement? That does happen at times, even when we have the right focus.

Often, a distraction is needed to overcome the lying symptoms. In my thinking, at this point, is that I'm already healed. I'm simply not able to recognize the improvement at the moment. Here is a perfect example of that.

In March 2018, just before "Unlocking" was published. I woke up to my left foot being bruised, swollen and extremely painful. All of my toes appeared to be broken. Tears were streaming down my face. It was pure agony. Since I'm already healed, I shoved my foot into the shoe but couldn't tie it. I limped to the car heading to work, in tremendous pain. It's a two-hour drive to Knoxville, TN. My mindset is I'm already healed. Therefore, there has to be improvement. For an hour I could not honestly say there was any improvement. I make my regular coffee stop at a Hardy's. Getting out of the car, I purposefully put all my weight on that foot, tremendous pain hits, tears come streaming down my face. A little lady comes running up to me and asks, "Are you ok?" My statement is, "Yes, I am in pain, but I am healed. Thank you." I know I seem crazy, but that was my response. I get my cup of coffee and head back towards the car. Right before reaching the car I slam my foot on the ground! Then, sitting down, suddenly my toes are moving. That told me that the swelling had suddenly gone down. Thank you, Jesus. I drive the rest of the way to Knoxville and pull into my first dealership.

There's a sixty-pound air compressor that I have to get out of the car. My focus is on getting it out of the car. As soon as I grab it, all the pain leaves. From that moment on my foot is good, no more problems. Thank you, Jesus. It did take two hours. But a broken bone healed in two hours is still a miracle.

Holy Spirit is giving life to my body, therefore there is no doubting or questioning, whether the healing would occur. I did not deny that there was anything wrong. There was no trying to prove that I was a "He-Man." I did carry on as normal, because I'm already healed. My focus was only on recognizing improvement. Neither did I deny "bravely" that I was in pain.

My main point is that no matter the circumstance, I am already healed. Therefore, my expectation is already set on recognizing the improvement. I'm not putting off my expectation. The time is now. I'm not questioning anything. My focus is on the fact that Holy Spirit is giving my body life. There were no excuses. I wasn't trying to get healed. I was not checking for sin as a reason or looking for something blocking my healing, none of those things.

My main point is my core belief: I'm already healed so there has to be improvement. My body isn't the gauge. Holy Spirit inside of me is and He's healthy. So am I.

Did you notice the two distractions that I needed to have in order to recognize the improvement? They were slamming my foot on the ground and lifting up the air compressor. These were distractions that enabled me to recognize the improvement. We'll discuss that in more detail later.

This is my **stern disclaimer time. Don't be stupid.** Any time I do something that could be considered stupid, it comes naturally through the Holy Spirit. I didn't sit there and plan to do it, nor do I do it as an "act of faith". These things are done because I know I'm already healed. There is no hesitation or fear. These actions happen naturally. Don't even do something with the line of thought, "If I do this, I'll be healed." Your thought process is wrong to begin with.

If you need to see a doctor, see a doctor. If you need to go to the emergency room, go. There is no shame in that, nor is it a lack of faith. We are all growing and maturing as we walk this path called life. Stay alive long enough to grow and mature into this truth I'm teaching. It does no good to deny yourself a doctor if you die in the process.

10 A LIE IS LIE

A lie is a lie, is a lie. A friend lies to you multiple times. Once you discover the lie, then the statement is dismissed completely. When healing is involved people walk about confronting the lie. "You lying symptoms, leave my body now". Let's get real. You are paying more attention to the lie than to the truth. This means what? The lying symptoms then become stronger than the truth that you are healed. Grab a cup of coffee, it's about to get very blunt!

The biggest problem is within us. This chapter is just about being honest with ourselves. We must be convinced that the symptoms are truly a lie. Then, we will no longer shadow box with the symptoms. What we think about the most is what we feel is the strongest. The lie then becomes the truth. We won't admit to it knowing that scriptures say Jesus bore our sicknesses. We are afraid to say scriptures are wrong (how many preachers dance around that one verse?). Yet, because we think sickness is normal, our actions reflect that. Bad is good, good is bad, and the truth is a lie.

The ultimate lie that is believed is that sickness is normal, unavoidable, it's going to happen. You are already heads above most, you do believe that God heals. I also think that most reading this book do believe that sickness should not be normal and it is not unavoidable. My friend, I'll even go as far as to say that you've seen people healed and you yourself have been healed from some things. Recognize that and Praise God for it. YAY! You are totally awesome! That much you are so correct on.

Here's where we do miss the boat. We concentrate too much on the lie. We command sickness to go. We speak to the symptoms, all the while not realizing that we're making that lie stronger in our minds. Many of you have been successful in doing it that way. In fact, I've done that as well.

If you are suffering from symptoms, you don't need to do something that draws your focus to the symptoms. We are well aware of the symptoms. We feel them, they slow us down, and they drain us of our energy. We speak to the body part, "pain in the leg, leave now." This is good if it is a new symptom, just starting up. It is resisting the devil. But at some point, it becomes a trap. We are then spending all of our time pointing ourselves right to the lie.

This is especially true of long-term paralysis. We command the body part to be loosened. Then, we look at it still not moving. Then, we switch to telling demons to leave... still not moving. All the while the lying symptom becomes stronger and stronger in our mind. We will even say that it's a lying symptom, but that's not what we really mean anymore.

I challenge you, find your shadow and start trying to hit it. Within a few minutes, you'll get tired and haven't accomplished anything. That is what we're doing when we are continually commanding symptoms to go, especially for long term illness. Pretty soon, the symptoms become a stronghold in the mind. We get frustrated more and more. We may even admit we must have unbelief, but we don't understand why. I believe and I've even seen other people healed. Yet, this symptom isn't going.

Think about it. From birth, we are shown to be aware of our body. We become super sensitive to the slightest changes in our bodies. Our friends will ask, "how are you doing?" In other words, how are the symptoms. Our doctors ask, "What are your symptoms?" Our friends and relatives keep asking, "What are the doctors saying?" Then, we have to repeat everything the doctor told us. We see commercials telling us to have our body tested regularly for this, that, and the other. Have you had your yearly breast exam?

We are inundated with being sensitive to the symptoms. Then, to top it all off, we call prayer lines, prayer boards, prayer groups where everyone is asking for the symptoms. So, we tell them. After we tell them what our symptoms are then they pray over it, the prayer is very likely begging God to heal the sickness, or commanding the sickness or devils to leave. Then we ourselves go to war against the symptoms. We are commanding them to leave. Do you see how all the attention is drawn to the symptoms?

Be encouraged though. I was healed in spite of all of this and without the knowledge I now have. The healing ministry has come a long way in just a short period of time. The commanding disease and devils away is a good starting point. In fact, it is how I got healed, by commanding the symptoms away. I am not knocking it. In reaching unbelievers or those who don't believe in healing, it is very effective. But for those who already believe in healing and have a long term or serious illness, it becomes ineffective.

We've lost sight of where our focus should be. How do we get rid of evil? Through truth. The sword of the Spirit is truth. Paul doesn't tell us to focus on evil, but on things of good report. Things that are Holy, pure, and of good account.

> *Finally brethren, whatsovever things are true, whatsoever things are honest, whatsoever things are just, whatsoever things are pure, whatsoever things are lovely, whatsoever things are of good report; if there be any virtue, and if there be any praise, think on these things. (Phillippians 4:8)*

When we are seeking healing for ourselves we should be focused on truth and the renewing of our minds to the truth, not on the lie. Think of it in these terms. We are fighting sickness which is negative with the lie of sickness which is actually two negatives. It is akin to Satan casting out Satan. This is what happens when we are so focused on the disease or injury. Jesus never did that. In fact, in most instances He used the affirmative, not the negative. Oh, I'm getting so scientific here, even using math. Lord forgive me.

If the command is to get up and walk, what is that saying? It is saying that you can get up and walk. How about telling the man with the withered hand to stretch his hand out? That is saying he can stretch his hand out. The blind man, what was Jesus telling him? By saying go wash the mud off at the fountain. He was saying that he could see, once the mud was off, all affirmative statements. Pick up your mat and go home. Do you see the difference? Instead of fighting a lie by commanding the lie, we use the spiritual reality truth that we are healed. Then, we are effectively renewing our mind to the truth and not confirming the lie.

In order for you to see your healing, it really just takes a few tweaks in the way we think. It is renewing our mind to the truth. Often, we get so focused on the fight that the truth is forgotten. We fight for our healing instead of having it.

Going back to the formula that was introduced in "Unlocking," belief plus expectation equals acknowledging our healing. The believing part is the unquestionable fact that we are already healed because Holy Spirit is giving life to our body. He is always affirming this. Yet, we don't hear Him because our fighting the symptoms is drowning His voice out. Fighting the "lying symptoms" and yelling and screaming at the lies, in many cases, is only reaffirming the lies. Throughout the time of being paralyzed, Holy Spirit kept telling me to get up and walk, I just wasn't hearing Him.

I want to encourage you to recognize the lying symptoms for what they are: a lie. Once we recognize the lie, we can then start believing the Truth. The words then I am healed start sounding like the truth and less of a lie. This is because I am no longer saying I'm healed, but thinking my symptoms are saying no I'm not. We can then be able to recognize improvement. Because we are no longer being contradictory and calling the truth a lie and the lie, the truth.

Oh, yeah. Gotta make a jabbing point here. Nothing annoys me more than when people state, "I'm healed in the Spirit." Straight up that's a cop out. It is Holy Spirit who is giving life to your mortal body. By saying that, you are stating that He is not doing His job. I'm healed "in the spirit" because Holy Spirit hasn't healed my body. Just recognize the lie from the truth. Be encouraged! Holy Spirit is giving life to your body. Our only part in it is to recognize and acknowledge that truth. We have everything we need. It's Him inside of us and He has already achieved it.

11 IT DOES APPLY TO YOU

It's four o'clock in the morning. I'm just sitting here asking Holy Spirit the next chapter, a chapter that will throw some cold water onto a person's face and wake them up. This chapter comes straight out of love and compassion. I want you to get some ice water, put it in the largest glass possible, and pour it on yourself. Please don't use coffee! That would burn you. Then, I'd have to pray for you to be healed. People are people. I would guess that most of you at some point just skip over sections and say, "That doesn't apply to me." If you're reading this book, **it does apply to you.** We rationalize things, so it appears to ourselves that it doesn't apply. This works both ways, on the good stuff and bad stuff.

In the last paragraph of the last chapter, I'll bet ninety percent of you have said "I'm healed in the spirit." Yet you won't recognize that my next statement after that is true. In that statement, we are denying all responsibility and putting it on Holy Spirit. In the same fashion, many of you after reading the book will say, "Good book, Tony." But Tony, I've done everything you've said and I'm still not healed. Part of the solution is always recognizing the problem. Don't turn this into condemnation, everything I'm saying applied to me while I was paralyzed. It also, to varying degrees, has applied to myself while I was on the journey to learning how to teach healing.

Neither I nor you are healed unless we believe we are healed. If we are still experiencing symptoms, then we aren't believing that we are healed.

I'm sorry, that is just the bottom line Truth. If I believe the symptoms over the fact that we're already healed, then I'm still sick. There are ministries that teach healing is all on the one praying. That is just wrong. I was not healed until I recognized and acknowledged that I was healed. What I'm truly believing is what manifests in my body, point blank. Hopefully, with this book, I'm furthering your understanding and will show you what causes us not to believe we're healed and provide you ways to overcome this unbelief. In fact, whenever I say that we are already healed, many of you will balk at me and point to the world and say, "See? you're wrong." There's still sickness in the world. There is because we don't believe we're already healed so we point to the sickness as proof. **That's Unbelief.**

"I'm not afraid," is such a common statement. As soon as I mention fear, nope not me. "Tony that doesn't apply to me". Meanwhile, there's rivers of sweat pouring off your forehead, you're quivering, and saying, "I don't want to die."

Why did you go to the doctor in the first place? Out of fear! You saw or felt something and were worried that something is wrong with your body. Fear happens, then through the Holy Spirit, we come into peace. We don't embrace fear. We reject it. Part of rejecting fear is recognizing it for what it is. "I just ate some chicken that tasted funny. I'm worried that it will cause me to get sick." That's fear! "My wife isn't home on time, I'm anxious something happened." That's fear!

We, as a society, are so full of fear! This is why we need Holy Spirit. The fear disorders that abound are unreal, especially among believers.

Here is a fact that I am very proud of for the body of Christ. We are starting to recognize fear and not be afraid to ask for help in that matter! It isn't being afraid that is shameful. It is not recognizing it or not seeking divine help for it.

When I mentioned Holy Spirit telling me throughout my healing journey that I was healed, most of you skipped over, ignored or rationalized it away instead of applying to yourself. "Holy Spirit ain't said that to me." He has. You just haven't heard him correctly. Notice, when I stated, I didn't realize it at that time. These things are stated so you can recognize that He is indeed always speaking to you. Be sensitive to it. Then, the ability to recognize will come.

One of my favorites and I think most helpful chapters of "Unlocking" is the chapter on the "Control Center" called "the Brain." From my point of view, it is the most ignored chapter of the whole book. Yet, applies to every single one of us.

Why are you scratching your head? You think I woke up on the wrong side of the bed? Talking about fear, what we eat controls nearly every facet of life. Yet, very few people acknowledge that we choose what we eat out of fear. We look to food to be our healer. I'm being completely serious. It is one of the least discussed chapters when it is the most important. Even among those who believe in healing, they are fearful of what they eat! Our first solution is food. Even those of us who believe in healing will offer herbal or organic remedies to others first.

Here's all I ask. Recognize the tendency to say that something doesn't apply to me. This does take on many forms which includes rationalizing. The majority of the time, we don't even recognize that we're doing this. This isn't a blame game just pointing out one part of what most of us are guilty of. Learn to see this behavior and stop it.

A friend of mine and myself were having a phone conversation. He had read, loved, and gotten a lot of revelation from "Unlocking". He had been healed of many of his physical ailments. He was struggling in one area. Actually, for a number of weeks, he had done quite well. Then came two bad days in a row that he wasn't understanding. "What had happened?" I asked. "Where was your expectation at? Are you looking for improvement?" We talked for a while, then I start blabbering.

He prays for the sick just like I do. I mention that seeing healing for yourself is the same process used when praying for others. In my mind, that person is already healed, even long before I came along. I am expecting improvement for them, then I recognize and acknowledge that improvement for them. This is the whole reason most of us ask for a pain level, so we can notice the improvement. When there is improvement, we point it out to them. Then they can see that indeed they are healed. It is the same process for us.

While I'm stating this, the light bulb goes off. Suddenly, he realized the day before the symptoms came back, he'd been doing some vigorous work. He thought to himself that he'd pay for it the next day because he was pushing himself too hard. He confided in me that often, his thought was that he'd better not overdo the physical exertion.

What was he expecting to happen? His thought was that it is normal to experience pain due to physical exertion. Therefore, the problems returned. He was anticipating the pain's return. This is common and that's where we need to renew our minds.

It was actually that phone conversation that encouraged me to write this book. That story is a great lead in to the next chapter. It is actually a great example of how easily we step on the wrong path.

My friend thought that his expectation was in fact in that he was completely healed. He had been looking for improvements and finding them until his expectation shifted. Without realizing it, because it is our human experience that when we overwork ourselves our muscles will be in pain, he got what he expected to happen.

As soon as this realization hit, the back pain left which is what we're going to talk about in this upcoming chapter. The main thing that causes unbelief is our physical senses telling us we're not healthy. How do we overcome our body telling us we're sick? I'm already healed, but my body is saying no I'm not.

The answer to that question is paramount. Let's make sure you're up to speed. Holy Spirit is giving life to your body, therefore you are healed, now you are looking to recognize improvements, to be able to acknowledge that you are healed. At this time, you may not be able to recognize the improvements, correct? Here's the simple answer: a distraction is then needed to overcome what the physical senses are telling you.

Remember the four miracles only the Messiah could perform? This is the only thing that I use from those individual healings. Many of those healings the person had no faith of being healed that we can tell. The reason is, at that time, they were incurable. Even the priests couldn't see those things healed.

The reasons for Jesus' actions were a means of distraction. With my own healing from the broken foot, I needed a distraction in order to recognize the improvement. With myself, the pain was so excruciating, that it was overwhelming me.

The distractions in my case were two-fold slamming my foot on the ground and picking up the air compressor. Jesus used the mud in the eyes of the blind man. Think of this. You're blind. You hear the person standing in front of you spitting. Then, all of the sudden you feel mud being put on your face. Huge distraction! Then, you're told to wash the mud off in the fountain. There was actually lot's going on with this.

This was on a Sabbath day for starters. The distance the man had to walk meant he was walking farther than what was allowed on a sabbath day. Can you even imagine what the man was thinking? Yeah, so this man is thinking that the Pharisees going to have him stoned to death! That is a huge distraction. His thoughts were on anything but am I going to be healed. Then you've got the deaf, dumb, and blind man. Jesus uses the wet willy finger in the man's ear. Which the man would've felt. That in itself would be a distraction.

A distraction interrupts the brain's and the soul's focus. The brain is now busy sending out other information and relaying it to the person's soul or mind. Both the brain and the mind are then busy doing other things. The hold that the physical senses has on that person is then weakened. Then, we can recognize improvement. This is huge in seeing people and ourselves healed.

There are many different forms of distractions. Just telling a person to get up and walk can be one form of distraction. Words of knowledge are also very helpful. This is when Holy Spirit shows us something we have no way of knowing. Words of knowledge both increase expectation and are a distraction at the same time. Simple ordinary things such as waking up can be a distraction because the brain is groggy and not running at full speed. Peter pulling up the lame man at the gate called beautiful was a distraction. The man's brain would've gone into a shock mode, long enough for the man to recognize that he was in fact standing. I've also done that quite a few times and *my disclaimer on not being stupid is appropriate here.*

Another form of distraction is emotionally charged situations. Anger is one of those. A sudden emotional outburst can be a very effective distraction. This totally overwhelms the physical senses. Then, the person can recognize their healing. In order for a distraction to be effective, it should not be planned out or given a lot of thought. When I slammed my foot on the ground there was no thinking about it. The grabbing of the air compressor was less of a distraction. But I was so focused on grabbing it, that action became an opportunity for me to able to recognize the healing.

12 MYSTERY REVEALED

The beginning of things was the Cross, this was when Christ took the poison out of this world. We can't stop there. We have to recognize and acknowledge the solution being poured into the world. We can't even stop there. The gift of the Cross is Holy Spirit in us.

There is now no mystery that hasn't been unsealed. We have the mind of Christ within us. The more we recognize this, the closer we come to living in the fullness of Christ. Healing is just the beginning of what lies below the surface. Let's do a coffee break while I make myself some breakfast.

The more that we are aware of Holy Spirit is one spirit with us, therefore giving life to our bodies, the more we will be able to recognize our bodies changing and becoming perfectly healthy. Then, not only will we be healed, but we'll start relying more on Christ's Spirit and rely less on our physical senses. When we rely less on physical senses, then we are walking more by the Spirit of Christ. The starting point is knowing there has to be improvement. We can't look to our bodies to see *if* there is improvement. We have to look knowing the improvement is there.

This is like being in a dark tunnel, we've got the choice to look at the darkness that is all around us. The darkness is our decaying mortal body and the sickness. When we are looking at the darkness, we're paralyzed with fear. Then, we do not take a step forward because we don't know which way forward is. This is what happens when we don't realize that Holy Spirit is in us and active.

All of the sudden, we recognize a glimmer of light. We realize where the entrance to the tunnel is. The light is Holy Spirit in us and the improvement in our bodies. When we focus only on the light, then we start seeing that light becoming brighter and brighter with each step. We're no longer even noticing the darkness. Suddenly, we're at the entrance bathed in light. This light is both the complete healing of our bodies and a deeper realization of Holy Spirit in us.

The more we realize Holy Spirit is one with us, the less the physical realities can affect us. We are now sons of God and truly spiritual beings. We are complete in Him and we start acting like it. We then are a light to others, spreading light to the outside world, guiding others to be bathed in the light of Holy Spirit within us. This is the path that my original healing took me on.

We can use healing to start down the path to light. Where now we have more than Adam and Eve did, we have completeness within ourselves. We can now interact with the physical world, without it affecting us, but now we can affect the realities of the physical world.

After Christ was resurrected, He was the first born of the integration of God into the human spirit. When we are reborn into Christ, we are exactly as He is now. We already have it, but because of the distraction of physical realities, we have not been able to realize this. Our focus has been in reaction to the physical world therefore we have missed out on maturing into sons of God. This is the same with healing. We have been distracted by the physical symptoms, thereby not being able to recognize that we are healed. This is also why Paul mentions the union between husband and wife. The physical things are meant to lead us into the spiritual reality. Yet, we miss this and stay stuck on the physical things.

A man and a woman start dating and become familiar with one another. This was Jesus coming into the world. He was introducing us to the Father in heaven. This man and woman decide to spend their lives together. There is a celebration we call a wedding, a union.

Our union with Christ actually happened after the destruction of the temple of Jerusalem in 70 A.D. This incident showed that the solution had been injected into mankind. The dating ritual which was the Law of Moses had been successfully maneuvered by Christ, so we could become the bride of Christ. We are fully integrated into Him.

With the physical marriage of man and wife, although they are completely unified, they have to become familiar with one another. They are now living together. For the first time, everything is brand new and different than it was when they were dating. There are arguments, trials, things that have to be overcome as they learn about one another. Slowly over time, they start acting as one person. They start being able to know each other's thoughts without verbal communication. They start to know how the other would react to any given circumstance because they have experienced each other's reactions. Now, they can confidently answer for the other person. They know what their spouse would do in any situation.

This is true of Our integration as the bride of Christ both as being the body of Christ and individually. It starts out on the individual level, and then spreads to the corporate body. For this book, we are talking about the at the individual level.

When we accepted Christ, we became one with Him, yet we didn't know how to communicate with Him. We don't realize that we are truly one with him. We get sick. We than start looking for someone outside of our union that has more maturity with Christ. We become reliant on them instead of building our own personal relationship with him. It would be like a young couple seeking a marriage counselor. The marriage counselor is there to help unify the spouses together. This is perfectly acceptable for a period of time. It becomes unacceptable, however, when the couple decides, instead of communicating with each other, they move the counselor in with them.

With healing that's been what's happened, instead of learning and teaching that Holy Spirit is in us, we can first be healed, made whole through Him, giving life to our mortal bodies. We instead teach go find someone to do it for us. Then, instead of getting to the point we know and actively communicate with Holy Spirit within ourselves, we become reliant on an outside party. Please don't misunderstand me. We should all be praying for the sick. We should indeed be that counselor unifying the spouses together. The problem is, when someone doesn't get healed, they keep looking outside of Holy Spirit within themselves. This is what this book has been about: That you realize that He is within you, actively taking care of you, and always healing you. As more individuals see their own healing, it will spread to the body of Christ. Then, we can be more focused on bringing unbelievers into the fold because the fold is now healthy. Because the individuals within the fold are divinely healthy, that in itself will attract those outside the fold into the fold.

Everything about the unification of the Spirit of Christ into our spirit is about life. Fighting against the physical nature of things keeps us away from actively knowing we have life already. We must tweak our thinking away from the fight to the resting in God. Part of actively knowing that we are in His Rest is knowing the integration of ourselves being sons of God is complete. There is nothing stopping us from having that rest now.

Overall, we have the mindset that we have to fight evil, both at the corporate and individual levels. A fight means that there is opposition. There is still evil in the world, but no opposition. Good in the form of Jesus has conquered evil and that goodness (Jesus), now has all authority both in heaven and on Earth. When we rest knowing that has been accomplished, we can then speak from a position of true authority. There is no longer anyone that can oppose this authority. Yes, evil does still exist on this Earth and there are demons. But none can oppose He who is in authority. We're not fighting evil. We're spreading truth, which is life, and life more abundantly. I know it sounds like double talk but it's not. Let's try this a different way.

Adam, having dominion of the Earth, chose the physical nature of things. Therefore, good and evil were born. Man's very nature became both good and evil. Christ came as a man, and overcame evil with good. Man's spirit is now unified with God's Spirit. Jesus is now the ultimate authority over the Earth. There is no questioning that and therefore, no more opposing nature. There is no authority that can now accuse mankind of being both good and evil. We point straight to Jesus who makes us holy. All of this being true, now we can spread the goodness of God throughout the world. At one time there was opposition that could accuse mankind, until Jesus.

Our focus now is on the unification of man and God's Spirit so there is no fighting, only resting. It is in that rest that goodness now overcomes evil. No more fighting to see which nature of man rules good or evil. Now, we replace the evils done in this world with the goodness of God. While there is evil on Earth there is no more opposition. We need only focus on spreading the Love of Christ that overcame man's evil nature.

God's rest then simply becomes a matter of knowing there is no opposition. So, when something appears to be wrong with my body, the physical nature of things, these symptoms are conquered so death is replaced with life. When I pray for someone, I am resting in this fact. I am, therefore, speaking life into that person with no opposition. All the other person has left to do is to acknowledge life.

I use the word Life that represents all that is good with abundance. We can say with all truth that we are now manifested sons of God.

> *But as many as received him, to them gave he power to become the sons of God, even to them that believe on his name.(John 1:12)*

> *For as many as are led by the Spirit of God, they are the sons of God. (Romans 8:14)*

This has already happened. We can walk in its fullness while we are on the Earth. We don't have to wait around. This life is about coming into the full stature of Christ while on this Earth NOW.

> *Till we all come in the unity of the faith, and of the knowledge of the Son of God, unto a perfect man, unto the measure of the stature of the fulness of Christ. (Ephesians 4:13)*

This scripture is in fact stating that as individuals we can come to the fullness of Christ, what we need to do is bring everyone else to that fullness, to the knowledge of the Son of God which means knowing that we are now fully integrated with God. When we get that as individuals, we'll start walking in it.

Then, as we one by one come to walk in it, we can all enjoy walking in the fullness of Christ. The more we walk in it, the more others will join us then the more we can truly walk in the fullness of what was already accomplished. This means in its entirety divine health now, interacting with the physical reality without being overwhelmed by the physical reality. We can have God's rest today.

> *For he that is entered into his rest, he also hath ceased from his own works, as God did from his. Let us labour therefore to enter into that rest, lest any man fall after the same example of unbelief. (Hebrews 4:10-11)*

That rest is freedom from the natural physical order of things whose end is death. Knowing that God has provided us with all things in this physical world now, we are lacking in no good thing. All we have to do is believe this. This is why it is so important to know that you are one spirit with the Lord. That you are a fully integrated son. We do have to grow and mature into this. There is no one that I know of that has the full realization of this. That is why unity to the faith is so important.

Healing and divine health are a monumental step to achieving this fullness. It is the process of learning that the physical nature of things no longer has a hold on us. This includes being limited by the needs of the body. Jesus is the tree of life, the Bread of Life, the Water of Life, the Vine. Christ in us makes us able to not be conformed to the physical boundaries of this life. We haven't even scratched the surface of the spiritual realities available to us while on Earth.

Healing is a stepping stone into living in the Spirit. It is a step into true reliance on Holy Spirit. Let's do a little recap just to make sure that you realize how simple it is to have your healing. Holy Spirit is giving life to our mortal body therefore all we need to do is recognize the improvement that has to be there, no question marks. Then, the symptoms will melt away. We'll be able to acknowledge our full healing, then at some point we'll encounter less and less health problems. The less reliant we are on our physical senses, the more we'll walk in divine health. The less sensitive we are to our physical body, the more sensitive we will be to Holy Spirit inside of us. The more we hear His speaking life within us, the less we will fear, because we know He is giving life into every situation where our physical life is concerned.

The remaining chapters in this book are going to talk about wrong beliefs about healing. Even though if you've read and understood, in all the previous chapters, all the wrong beliefs should have been discounted merely by focusing on who Jesus is in us. Holy Spirit is in us. Therefore, there is nothing that can stop healing. Healing is not contingent on our actions, only on the full integration of His Holy Spirit in us.

13 ANGEL ARMIES

I'm the one that needs the coffee now! Let me go on record as stating that there are angels and there are demons. Let me also go on record, we pay entirely too much attention to them. Before I totally tick everyone off, let me explain.

There is a specific reason I'm mentioning angels. There are many methods concerning healing that have come around involving angels. People are infatuated with angels and many think we become angels upon death. This is not true, we are higher than angels. Let's take a short look at angels to clarify their involvement with healing.

> *Are they not all minstering spirits, sent forth to minister for them who shall be heirs of salvation? (Hebrews 1:14)*

Angels are spiritual beings who serve Christ, the King of kings. Yet, when you take an in-depth look, there are very few accounts of actual interaction between man and angels. Most of the accounts are specifically in regard to Jesus.

In the Old Testament, God used angels as messengers between Himself and man. Angels were also used to protect God's servants. There is only one account in all of scripture of any involvement with healing whatsoever.

> *For an angel went down at a certain season into the*

> *pool, and troubled the water: whosoever then first after the troubling of the water stepped in was made whole of whatsoever disease he had. (John 5:4)*

The long and short of angels, in my opinion, is in the Old Testament before Christ came. They existed so God could communicate with specific people. We have the instance of Lot in Sodom:

> *And there came two angels to Sodom at evening; and Lot sat in the gate of Sodom.... (Genesis 19:1b)*

Lot didn't even know they were angels. To him they were just travelers. With the account of Abraham and Sarah this is the same. Remember, it was Moses writing the account. So, he's writing it retrospectively.

By all accounts, I don't believe that Abraham knew at the time they were angels visiting. In both cases with Lot and Abraham, they are assuming they are men. They go about as was custom in caring for them, urging them to rest, and preparing a meal for them.

This is the case with most in angelic interactions in scriptures. It is retrospectively that people recognize they were being visited by angels. There are only nine times at the most when angels visit humans in angelic form and the person knew they were angels. Those times had nothing to do with healing. They were directly involving Jesus.

> *And there appeared unto him an angel of the Lord standing on the right side of the altar of incense. (Luke 1:11)*

> *And the angel said unto her, Fear not, Mary; for thou hast found favour with God. (Luke 1:30)*

> *And, lo, the angel of the Lord came upon them, and the glory of the Lord shone round about them: and they were sore afraid. (Luke 2:9)*

And, behold, there was a great earthquake: for the angel of the Lord descended from heaven, and came and rolled back the stone from the door, and sat upon it. (Matthew 28:2)

And while they looked steadfastly toward heaven as he went up, behold, two men stood by them in white apparel; (Acts 1:10)

But the angel of the Lord by night opened the prison doors, and brought them forth, and said... (Acts 5:19)

And the angel of the Lord spake unto Philip, saying, Arise, and go toward the south unto the south unto the way that goeth down from Jerusalem unto Gaza, which is desert. (Acts 8:26)

And behold, the angel of the Lord came upon him, and a light shined in the prison: and he smote Peter on the side, and raised him up, saying Arise up quickly. And his chains fell off from his hands. (Acts 12:7)

For there stood by me this night the angel of God, whose I am, and whom I serve... (Acts 27:23)

There were also two times with Jesus, and this is not considering the Old Testament times with Jacob's ladder, Elijah, and Elisha. I did not include those accounts, because they were before Christ's coming when God used angels a little more frequently. It was still very rarely that they were angels in their angelic form.

The rest of the accounts of angels were by dreams or visions. In all these accounts, healing is nowhere in the picture. Our society has such a thirst for the angelic world and is completely infatuated with the angelic world. Yet, scriptures do not support this infatuation.

Scriptures are extremely vague about angels for a reason. Let angels do what they are told to do by Jesus. Leave them alone. They have nothing to do with you being healed. There is no body parts room in heaven or any of that nonsense. We do not command the angel armies. Jesus does. People that see angels in angelic form should take extreme caution. People that I hear bragging about being visited often in their angelic form, I pray for them. Because a close study of scriptures shows it rarely happens.

Five times it directly involved the birth of Jesus. Dreams and visions of angels were a little less rare, but still very rare. Please don't misunderstand me. We can all operate in the prophetic and we can all have dreams or visions. Just make sure that they're legitimate.

Here's the bottom line. We can all have an intimate relationship with Christ. He now communicates with us personally through Holy Spirit in us. The Father in heaven no longer needs to send angels to communicate with us because He is in us. We also have Paul's warning. It is there for a reason.

> *Let no man beguile you of your reward in a voluntary humility and worshiping of angels, intruding into those things which he hath not seen, vainly puffed up by his fleshly mind. (Colossians 2:18)*

Neither Jesus nor any of His Apostles ever ordered angels' involvement with either healing or in casting out demons. You have what you need for your healing, Holy Spirit inside of you. Fleshly mind being the physical senses which the imagination uses, instead of looking for an encounter with an angel, look for an encounter with Holy Spirit who is speaking to you constantly.

> *Be not forgetful to entertain strangers: for thereby some have entertained angels unawares. (Hebrews 13:2)*

This is the most common occurrence of being visited by angels. We don't know they are angels until after the event. I have three experiences that would fall into this category. We do have angels all around us and they are ministering spirits. I do believe that they are here to protect us while we are growing and maturing into reliance on Holy Spirit. They are buffers for us as we learn and grow. I think even more so while we were unbelievers.

There are many events in my life that, looking back, I believe angels were responsible for my living through those events. You see, I don't discount angels at all like you were probably thinking. I just quit yearning for encounters with them, but recognize when they do happen and am grateful to the Father, Jesus, and Holy Spirit.

My favorite, though a little puzzling encounter, is when I had a job taking people to their medical appointments. I was at a hospital parking lot, waiting for my last client to be finished. I was parked on the far end of the hospital which was somewhat secluded. I could see the entrance to my left, but to my right there was nothing but woods about fifty feet deep. There was a path that went into a clearing and no other parked cars close to me. I noticed an elderly man walking towards me. He was using a walker at a very slow pace. My intention was to pray for him. He was at a distance of about five feet from my vehicle. I was about to approach him when I got a phone call from my boss. The phone call lasted less than a minute. I looked after hanging up and he was nowhere in sight. I'm puzzled at this point. Certainly, he couldn't have made it to that path. He had been moving very slowly. I went down the path. Then, checking out the clearing, he was nowhere around. It wasn't till later that day the thought occurred to me that he could've been an angel.

Another incident, which is disputable, was when I was asked to pray for a man that had a leg that had been amputated. He had a prosthetic on. No one to my knowledge knew him. He had asked prayer for phantom pain. I prayed for him, the pain left, then the thought occurred to me why stop there. I prayed for a new leg. Then, realizing that with the prosthetic leg being there the new one couldn't grow out, I asked him to take the fake leg off. He stated he'd have to go to the bathroom to take it off. About fifteen minutes later, he came out hollering, "Tony! Tony!" I hadn't given him my name. I looked. The fake leg was in his arms and he was standing on two legs.

The reaction by the leadership at the church was pathetic. They literally turned their backs on me and him. They wouldn't even acknowledge us. We left, and we were both angry. While walking to the parking, I went to say something to him and he was gone. There was no way he could've disappeared that quickly. What to make of that incident, I have no idea.

Then, there was the time when I was an atheist that a car went to run me over. All of a sudden, I feel something grab me and lift me up in the air. I was over twenty feet in the air and the landing was soft! That doesn't happen when you're that high in the air. The fella that had tried to run me over was terrified. That definitely was an angelic encounter as well.

My point with these examples is that there is angelic activity going on all around us. Recognize when they happen, but don't go overboard with trying to have the experiences on a willful level. Our focus should be on relying on Holy Spirit and operating at a higher level with the mind of Christ. The higher we're operating with the "mind of Christ," the less we'll need these experiences.

Think of it this way. In His Glorified body, does Jesus need the assistance of angels? Yet, in his glorified body they are all around Him. People that go around telling of angelic encounters in their angelic state are operating more by their physical senses and relying less on Holy Spirit. Elisha asked for his servant's sake for the Lord to let his servant see the angels around him, not for his own sake. What we think is being super spiritual, most of the time isn't. Normally it comes from us needing to see it to believe it.

As for angels being involved with healing or deliverance, it's the same thing, Jesus told us: to heal the sick, raise the dead, cleanse the lepers. He never told us to ask angels to do it. Get over it! I've seen and heard a lot of stuff about healing and deliverance that is just nonsense that doesn't have any scriptural backing whatsoever. Time to move onto the next chapter before I offend anyone else.

14 DEFEATED DEMONS

I'm in the habit of fighting lies with the Truth. It would take a whole book in and of itself to get rid of all the lies believed about demons. The Truth is, what applies to salvation applies to healing. What applies to healing applies to deliverance. In this book, I have spent very little time talking about demons or deliverance. The reason I haven't is because it's the same thing. Believe the lie, you get the lie. Believe the Truth, it is that Truth that sets you free. Time to get some more coffee brewed up. This is going to be a long chapter.

What is a demon or unclean spirit? A demon is spiritual being that carries a lie. How does it travel into us? Through our physical senses, they come in through the outside world, we then believe the lie. What is sin? A sin is anything contrary to God's Spoken Word. The Father always speaks life, never death.

> *But when he had turned about and looked on his disciples, he rebuked Peter, saying, Get thee behind me, Satan: for thou savourest not the things that be of God, but the things that be of men. (Mark 8:33)*

Jesus called Peter the accuser why? He answered that question with for thou savourest not the things that be of God, but the things that be of men. The whole conversation revolved around Jesus sacrificing Himself for the world. If Peter would have had his way, he would have chosen death for mankind. Jesus came to save the world, not destroy it. Had Jesus not taken the original sin unto

Himself, then all of mankind would have been destroyed. It is always a choice between thinking LIFE or DEATH, the TRUTH or the LIE. Let's look once again at the garden for the answer to what is a demon.

The evil that was released in the garden was by what or whom? The serpent is representative of the devil. We've got the tree of life on one hand, and the tree of knowledge of good and evil on the other. There were two choices. The first thing the serpent did was to point Eve to the things of men.

> ...*Yea, hath God said, Ye shall not eat of every tree of the garden? (Genesis 3:1)*

The serpent baited Eve by the question, drawing her physical eyes to the tree. He was twisting the truth and phrased it so that her attention was drawn to the tree of death. Then continues with the lie:

> *And the serpent said unto the woman, Ye shall not surely die:... (Genesis 3:4)*

It was at this time demons were born. How was the demon born? By the spoken word of the serpent which then drew her physical senses to the tree of death. The spoken lie was then brought into her by first her hearing, then seeing, touching, probably smelling, and finally tasting. Then, that would make demons the breath of a lie, or the spoken word is what gave breath to the lie. At any time, she could have switched her focus from the tree of death by looking at the fruit of the tree of life.

> *But every man is tempted when he is drawn away of his own lust, and enticed. Then when lust hath conceived, it bringeth forth sin: and sin, when it is finished, bringeth forth death. (James 1:14-15)*

The serpent was, therefore, a being that carried a lie. This is all demons are. They are not all-powerful beings that most would have you believe.

Notice in James, every man is tempted when he is drawn away of his own lust. The temptation comes from what is coming in from the physical senses. Then, we have the choice.

A person looks at porn and is being enticed by a spirit of this world. The idea that a demon has control over a person is a lie. If I'm delivering a person, then I am introducing Life and Truth into that person, I am casting out the lie which is exactly what we are to do. The person then has the choice to renew their mind to the Truth, that feeling loved doesn't come from watching porn, but comes from knowing the Love of God. Casting out demons is no different than seeing a person healed from cancer. The person is held captive in the sense that they know no other way to think.

The idea that a demon can resist being cast out is utter nonsense. There is no other way to say it. It is that individual knowing no other way to think. Once a person accepts the truth, then the lie is gone.

In my life, I've been that totally insane person. Before my healing, I was completely insane. During my forty-three years of life, I was at different levels of insanity. The types of insanity were from being on the outer fringe of being homicidal to severe post-traumatic stress disorder. I was addicted to almost anything and everything. I was also diagnosed as being a schizoid with extreme lack of compassion. I am speaking from experience.

I've also been the one that spoke with another voice, or how most Christians would view it as being possessed. This same person who happens to be me, was suddenly delivered of all these things as well in one, huge swoop. Thank You, Jesus! Then, I had to renew my mind or I would fall prey to those thoughts again.

We prefer to go Hollywood, imagining them as these creatures that can come and go into a person's body at will. They cannot come and go as they please, but they can control our actions to the degree we allow them to. Some food for thought: Give me a physical description of a demon that is in scriptures. Well? There aren't any because they are simply beings that carry a lie. If we imagine them as Hollywood creations, then we can come up with all kinds of rules and regulations to combat them. Most of these rules and regulations are fear based and are driven by what that minister has observed with their physical senses. Instead of simply giving the other person an injection of the cure, the cure is Truth. The Truth is the life-giving person of the Spirit of Christ.

Here's a thought-provoking scenario. What would have happened if Adam had commanded the serpent to leave, perhaps even by yelling, and screaming? The serpent would be gone, but the lie remained in Eve's thoughts. She would've at some other time grabbed the fruit, offering it to Adam once again.

However, what if Adam had said, "Eve look at the Tree of Life. See how much more luscious it looks? The fruit on it is bigger. See the juices coming out of it?" Eve looks at it, foaming at the mouth, and the crisis is diverted because now she is thinking of the correct fruit.

Let's take that scenario a step further. What if Adam had stood watch to make sure the serpent never came back. All of his focus is now on the "demon" snake. Anytime the snake comes, he's screaming at it to leave. Then, because of the noise, now there are more snakes. All Adam is doing now is screaming and hollering at the snakes. Meanwhile, the thought of the fruit is already in Eve's thoughts. Adam never injected the cure, so Eve grabs the fruit. Adam being tired, worn out, exhausted, gives up and takes the fruit.

This is exactly how we're conducting deliverance. We're screaming, hollering, and yelling for demons to leave. We never inject the Truth into people. All of our focus is on the lie, more lies come, and we are overwhelmed. The answer would be to put more focus on the Truth than on the lie.

With ourselves we do the same thing. We focus so much on the lies of the physical world that we become overwhelmed and never inject ourselves with the truth. The center focus of the deliverance ministry is sin. Every single aspect of deliverance is focused on sin. It is the Truth that sets people free, not sin or demons. So, why then are we so focused on them? Here's the cure: Holy Spirit in us giving life to our soul and body. It is the same as healing. There is no difference. The body of Christ is in jeopardy, because we think the solution is on fighting evil and sin. Christ being the answer, is left out of the equation. Oh, we're doing it "in the Name of Jesus." Yet, the cure of Christ in us is never injected.

Essentially, we have two types of deliverance ministries. There is the type that is saying, "Spirit of fear, I command you to leave! Leave now, you lying demon! I command you to leave now! You better leave now, you lying spirit! Please leave now, you little puny thing. I see you there sucking the life out my sister. So, leave now! Yes, I see you wrapped there on her spinal cord sucking the life out of her. Leave now! I plead the blood of Jesus over her!" Then there can be at times a manifestation through burping or whatever. Ok, you're delivered. This can go on for hours.

I'm putting it the way I've seen and heard it done, not to make fun of anyone, but so you can recognize the nonsense in this way. Jesus doesn't portray this, nor do the Apostles in Acts. There is not one time anyone states, "I plead the Blood of Jesus," in scripture. Not a single time anywhere in scripture. This type of deliverance is mostly ineffective. You can show me videos of the person manifesting, writhing around. But two days later, are they still free? In most cases, no, they aren't. In some cases, they are, but it's because that person renewed their mind to the Truth. This way is more scriptural than the second type.

Jesus does command demons out of a person. He is casting out the lie. This was before the Cross. Look after the cross: Peter and his shadow, Paul and his cloth… There is no screaming, hollering, or commanding. There is only the Spirit of Christ being released and freedom attained.

Remember please, this book is mainly for yourself being healed or delivered. This book is also Believer focused. During street ministry, the way I see people delivered is by introducing life and the Love of Christ. On the outside looking in, it would appear to be more like the commanding type of way. My attitude though is that the person is already made whole and set free. I'm just enabling them to be able to recognize it. I look at it no differently than I look at healing.

The second type of deliverance ministry is totally sin focused. This deals with generational curses and past sin. A large portion of this is counseling more than anything, a search for past sins that were unrepentant of. Ugh! The nonsense of it all. This type of ministry can take months, years, and often there is little if any progress made. This type deals with the legal rights of a demon to remain. Utter ignorance and nonsense.

There is one bright spot to this type of ministry. It does often focus on the Love of Christ. Let me interject something here. At least people in these ministries are looking to help people. I applaud them and there are successes. I do not hold any of them in contempt. I do, however, disagree with their methods.

Very few people talk about being self-delivered or show how one attains that. We come up with so many rules it makes it appear as if, in order to attain freedom, we must go to another human being in order to have freedom. Meanwhile, mental illnesses runs rampant with depression and bi-polar diseases on the rise.

The foundational truth remains the same as healing: the Holy Spirit inside of me is giving life to my soul. Therefore, I am healed/delivered. Now, I can recognize the improvement that is there. I can acknowledge my freedom from that spirit. Let's look at depression.

Depression is the lie coming in from the outside world through my physical senses that my life is without hope. I have no expectation of anything good coming to me in this life. Just like with my body, I'm not using my senses as the gauge. I'm not looking at the circumstances to determine whether my life is hopeless or not. I recognize the lie and confront it with the truth: Greater is He who is in me than he who is in the world. Therefore, my life is full of expectation and Holy Spirit is filling my heart with expectation of a full life. Now, I'm looking for the positive changes in my life. When I'm looking knowing that they're there, I will find them. Things will start to supernaturally change. Just like healing, I can ask Holy Spirit to point out the miraculous changes in my life.

Another example is when anger, depression, anxiety, panic attacks first start. I shift into stepping out of the situation. I can take a literal step backwards, stepping out of the negative spirit into the Spirit of Life. Now, I thank Holy Spirit that He has already released His peace into me. I then take a step forward, stepping into His peace. Once again, I can put all my focus into doing a task. Within minutes, I have the peace of Holy Spirit. This becomes an automatic response, relying on Holy Spirit and not on the outside world. I'm no longer fighting shadows but acknowledging the peace that is within me. In God's Kingdom of rest, I am resting in the fact that now, I'm a son of God. All my needs are taken care of. But it is an active not a passive way. I am eagerly anticipating or expecting to recognize changes. Therefore, the supernatural will happen. This is transformation happening by the renewing of your mind to the mind of Christ.

Here's another life example. Right now, there is a hurricane bearing down on the east coast. Hurricane Florence is coming in. I can holler and scream, "Demonic storm, you ain't landing here! You stay away and dissipate right now!" Or, I can do as Jesus did and speak peace, "Right now, I speak peace and calm over the weather. Peace. Be still."

Do you see the difference? One is a position of weakness, the other, from a position of strength. I am being active in both situations. The first way, I'm speaking not with the resolution, but actually acknowledging that the hurricane has power. Instead of injecting Truth, I'm upholding the lie. It's the same with any emotion. I have the choice to either recognize the Truth or the lie. Both are active, but one is actually creating expectation in the negative, not the things of God.

Paul did not focus on the demonic as we do at all. His focus was on who we are In Christ. He was not fighting the demonic. He was bringing life into all situations just as Jesus did. We can do the same: Recognize the lie, then inject the truth into the situation.

15 TRASH TRADITIONS

The Father's wisdom is all about life, not death. It's all about the freedom from death we have in Jesus. Anything we speak contrary to life, we're in agreement with death and the demonic. To look at a fellow human being saying, "God is teaching you a lesson to draw you in to Himself," is so demonic. That line of thought is even worse when it comes from someone who claims to be a leader in the body of Christ. That is perpetuating a lie which is no different than what the Pharisees did.

Making a list of rules that has to be checked off in order to attain healing or deliverance is just as abhorrent. My belief is to reveal Truth. The lie is then exposed. So, I don't teach a lot on the false beliefs of men. There are many good leaders that bring the lies of human traditions to the light. Yet, there will be a few even after they read this book because the bad traditions have been believed for so long. They will tack the traditions on to what I've spoken about, which will cause them to not be able to recognize their healing. Grab some coffee as we discuss the strongest traditions of men.

Here's a tradition: **God's Will is still a mystery of what He wants for individuals.** "You know, Tony, we just got to wait and see if God wants to take me from this Earth by cancer." This is also called God's Sovereignty or God controls everything that happens on Earth, that everything that happens on Earth is by God's design.

This is foolish, stupid, ignorant, utter nonsense, and did I say stupid. Who made the choice for you to go to work this morning? You did. Who made the choice for me to write this book? I did. Who chooses where you work? You did. Did you make the decision to eat breakfast the morning? If I get in my car and cut in front of someone causing a wreck, who's responsibility is that? That's correct. It would be mine, not God's responsibility. How about the second verse of The Lord's Prayer:

> *Thy kingdom come. Thy will be done in earth, as it is in heaven. (Matthew 6:10)*

Why did Jesus say to pray that prayer if The Father controls everything?

> *Today I call heaven and earth to record this day against you, that I have set before you life and death, blessing and cursing: therefore choose life, that both thou and thy seed may live:(Deuteronomy 30:19)*

Whose choice is it? Yours and mine. He even tells us which one to choose. He said to choose Life. Therefore, who's choice is it? If God's Will was automatically done, then why would Jesus tell us to pray that His Will be done on Earth? Right there in Deuteronomy God is telling us His Will, that you and your seed shall live. That is His Will and it isn't a secret. Let's look at Jesus when He asks what is it that you want? His answer was let it be done as you desire. Then we have John 10:10:

> *...I have come that they might have life, and that they might have it more abundantly.*

Come on now folks! It's all there in scriptures. There is no mystery in what God's Will is. The mystery is why humans keep choosing death. It is because we keep believing a lie. Then here comes the, *"Yeah, but..."* There is no, *"Yeah, but...,"* only Truth. Not in one place in the Gospels or the New Testament is there a '*but*' when it comes to healing. We have Jesus with the adulterous woman. By the Law of Moses, she should've been stoned. Which did Jesus support, life or death? Where did Jesus send that woman a disease? Did that clear up, that malicious lie? It is our choice whether to act by what our physical experiences show us and come up with excuses to support us believing a lie, or simply start believing the truth.

God allowed it, goes right along with this blasphemous belief. If God allowed it, then He wouldn't have sent us Jesus so we could be called sons of God. End of story. Hush right there. Just simply stop the nonsense.

Then, there's the argument that **there would be an overpopulation if everyone lived forever.** The Earth couldn't support it. Since He created Adam and Eve to live forever, He created the Earth to be able to support it.

I do apologize, if I seem a bit angry at this point. These wrong beliefs are the cause of people dying and it's those who claim to be Christians that spread these lies based on their physical senses.

God's decides when a person gets healed, or His Timing. This is another one of those beliefs that keep people sick. Does God decide when you leave for work? If you waited for God to turn the key, put the car in drive, etc., how long do you think you'll be waiting? Then, I suppose it would be God's fault for you getting fired because He didn't drive you to work. You laughed at that one, but I'm being serious.

When Paul was bitten by the poisonous snake, did he sit down in the grass and wait for God to decide when he'd be healed from the snake bite? No, he didn't. Paul knew he was healed and carried on as if nothing had happened. Jesus in his earthly ministry never told anyone to wait to be healed. It was always at that moment.

Then, someone will bring up with the ten lepers, or the man at the fountain that were healed on the way. So, think of it like this. They were all healed when they recognized they were healed. Plain and simple. We are healed when we believe that we are healed. That is just the truth. If we are waiting for something that has already happened, we'll keep waiting. It isn't Gods decision on when we recognize our healing, it's our decision.

Next, we've got Paul's thorn in the flesh, another "great mystery." We don't know what it was. Baloney! Paul states it straight out. They were messengers sent by Satan, the accuser, to bruise him. They were men that believed lies sent to slow the spreading of the message of the gospel of Christ.

> *And lest I should be exalted above measure through the abundance of revelations, there was given to me a thorn in the flesh, the messenger of Satan, to buffet me, lest I should be exalted above measure. For this thing I besought the Lord thrice, that it might depart from. And he said unto me; My grace is sufficient for thee: for my strength is made perfect in weakness. Most gladly therefore will I rather glory in my infirmities that the power of Christ may rest upon me. (2 Corinthians 12:7-9)*

When it is all taken in context, it is very clear what Paul was writing about. There is no mystery at all. The epistles are letters. There were no chapters, titles, or numbers. The context of what Paul is writing about starts back in chapter 11, verse 13. Then, starting in 11:23-29, Paul is listing what he went through.

> *Are they ministers of Christ: (I speak as a fool) I am more in labours more abundant, in stripes above measure, in prisons more frequent, in deaths oft. Of the Jews five times received I forty stripes save one. Thrice was I beaten with rods, once was I stoned, thrice I suffered shipwreck, a night and a day in the deep; In journeyings often, in perils by mine own countrymen in perils by the heathen, in perils in the city, in perils in the wilderness, in perils in the sea, in perils among false brethren; in weariness and painfulness in watchings often, in hunger and thirst, in fastings often, in cold and nakedness, besides*

those things that are without.

Paul first identifies who it was sent by: Satan not God. Then, a thorn in the flesh, meaning men. A simple search shows this phrase used twice which was persecution of the children of Israel by pagans. Honestly, you don't even have to do the search. Thorn in the flesh, in other words, a similar phrase that we use, "you're a pain in the butt."

Hello, it isn't hard to figure out. It was the persecution by men that Paul asked the Lord three times to take away. The Lord said, "In your weakness, I am strong." In other words, when you're going through this, I am with you in power. Paul confirms this by stating, "Therefore, I will glory in my weakness that the power of Christ may rest on me."

Paul was miraculously saved through each and every one of these events mentioned above. No one survived being stoned! Paul didn't either, he was raised from the dead on that occasion. Hello! That's the Power of Christ! Whippings weren't survivable either. A person that survived the initial whipping would suffer infection and die. He went through that five times. The Power of Christ truly rested on Paul. None of these events were survivable, including being shipwrecked. When he was shipwrecked, he was a prisoner of the Romans. If there was a ship going down the Roman soldiers would kill the prisoners so there was no way they could escape. Yet, Paul survived. Preachers that teach it was a "mystery illness," are denying the power of Christ and need our prayers. I am being very serious here. Take a moment and pray for the preachers that preach this falsely.

Let's not forget the book of Job. This has been long disputed, by many scholars. There should be no dispute. Did Job have the Holy Spirit within him? No. This was before Christ. Many Christians find false comfort in using Job thinking that they are being tested by God through Satan. This is no longer valid because of Christ. In fact, that isn't what was going on here either.

Job actually reveals several truths. Satan has to work through mankind. He can do nothing without a human being to work through. In this case, he used the Sabeans and Chaldeans. Also, Job shows that he saw God as both good and evil.

> *And said, Naked came I out of my mother's womb, and naked shall I return thither: The Lord gave, and the Lord hath taken away; blessed be the name of the Lord. (Job 1:21)*

> *What? Shall we receive good at the hand of God, and shall we not receive evil? (Job 2:10a)*

That is Job speaking and he thought the Lord had caused the evil. He saw God as both good and evil.

> *Job said, It may be they my sons have sinned, and cursed God in their hearts. (Job 1:3a)*

> *For the thing which I greatly feared is come upon me, and that which I was afraid of is come unto me. (Job 3:25)*

We get what we expect. Fear is not faith. At that time, the Earth was under Satan's jurisdiction. He was the accuser. Therefore, God had to remove the hedge of protection. Yet, God still protected his life. Then, in chapters 38 through 41, we find out the reason why Satan was able to afflict Job. It was out of pride and arrogance. In chapter 42, Job repents and then prays to God for the forgiveness of his friends. That is when everything is restored to him, double what he had lost. That part is important. If Job hadn't prayed, then his friends could have suffered worse than he had. This also shows that everything his friends had spoken was false, where many of the wrong teachings comes from with preachers using the words of Eliphaz, Bildad, and Zophar as if God had spoken it. The verse below proves that what Job's friends spoke was wrong.

> *And it was so, that after the Lord had spoke these words unto Job, the Lord said unto Eliphaz the Temanite, My wrath is kindled against thee, and*

against thy two friends: for ye have not spoken of me the thing that is right, as my servant Job hath. (Job 42:7)

In other words, in the book of Job, you can scratch out all the words of Job's three friends. Most of the book consists of those three speaking wrongly, advising, and accusing Job. Yet, preachers today use their words, and say that God said them. We had better pray for them as well.

To recap on Job, in that time-period, Satan had rule over mankind. Today, Christ Jesus has all authority. We now have Christ's Spirit in us, which places us above accusation. when we believe that truth, the plight of Job has nothing in common with us today. Unless you believe that lie, of course. Everything hinges on what you believe! If you believe a lie, then that is what you get. Believe the Truth, then that is what you get, Truth.

There are many, many false traditions of men. Suffice it to say that, if you are focused on the truth and having a deeper revelation of Christ in you, then you will avoid the many follies of man. Which is why the scope of this book is to unveil the truth. Then, you don't have to focus on the lies. If you focus on uncovering all the lies, then your time and energy is spent on the wrong thing and you won't be able to grow into maturity or into divine health.

The last lie that I'm going to cover is the lie that, **if you suffer tragedy, it is because you're traveling upstream against the devil and you have a target on your back.** New Christians are told that because you accept Christ the devil is going to target you and you'll suffer immensely. This is also believed by many of us who pray for the sick and see them healed. We then get into the mindset that because we are operating in the power of the Holy Spirit, the devil will target us for tragedy. It actually becomes "bragging rights." "Look at everything that I've done for God! The devil is trying to stop me." This is the wrong mindset and will actually set us up for more tragedies.

The spiritual mindset and the physical mindset are naturally at war with one another. Therefore, it isn't Satan that is personally targeting Christians. The bigger picture is this, our expectation becomes what we get. If we start expecting resistance, we get it.

There are two mindsets at work here: one that is saying that the devil only sends evil to believers, which is not true. Unbelievers and believers alike have horrible things happen to both themselves and their families. There is no difference in the evil that falls on people. I truly hate when I hear a preacher or anyone insinuating that the evil is only happening to Christians. It's a stupid statement. The same when I hear, "Well, the devils been on me today. I was going to pray for someone and had a flat tire. He's trying to stop me from praying for that person." **Or there's a revival going on and things are happening. The devil is trying to stop the revival. We're going to push on anyway and defeat the devil.** UGH! Stop it people.

When I was an atheist heading to a rock concert, bad things would happen as well! Or when I was going to go out to a bar, something would happen and put off my plans. So just quit with the arrogance and pride already!

Another example is sickness: Well, the devil put this on me because of the great things I was supposed to do for the Lord. Then, what about the unbeliever that has the same disease? Just stop it already!

The devil isn't what our focus should be on anyhow. I have the Holy Spirit in me, giving life to the situation. When I actively know that, then we make it through all the things that commonly happen to all humans. Here is the difference. Because Holy Spirit is in us and we actively believe that He is active, then:

> *Above all, taking the shield of faith, wherewith ye shall be able to quench all the fiery darts of the wicked. (Ephesians 6:16)*
>
> *Ye are of God, little children, and have overcome them: because greater is he that is in you, than he*

that is in the world. (1 John 4:4)

Behold, I give unto you power to tread on serpents and scorpions, and over all the power of the enemy: and nothing shall by any means hurt you. (Luke 10:19)

For whatsoever is born of God overcometh the world: and this is the victory that overcommeth the world, even our faith. Who is he that overcometh the world, but he that believeth that Jesus is the Son of God? (1 John 5:4-5)

You can dilute these verses down as much as you want to and use them for, well, someday when we're all in heaven. Or, you can use these verses to start walking on the Earth as sons of God now.

One last thing on this topic. Early on in my walk with healing, whenever someone would get healed, all havoc would break out at home. I would get a phone call from my wife in a panic. This went on for about a month. Then, the Lord drew me to the above scriptures and showed me that I had come to expect things to go crazy at home whenever there was a healing. This is often what happens, we start expecting the bad things to occur. We get what we expect to happen. This changed when I changed my expectation. I would simply remind myself that greater is He who is in me than he who is in the world. My family, my whole household, is protected. That is when things settled down.

16 FOOD OR HOLY SPIRIT

Super-hot topic where I'm in the bottom one percent! This chapter was added after this book was finished. I will tell you why. It's because we are too dependent on food. It is a stronghold of man's traditions so, I was compelled to write this chapter. There are two sides to every story, the far left and the far right. Then, there is God's stance on it. The far left is those that say you can eat anything without any responsibility. The far right says you are responsible for what you put into your body. After all, your body is the temple of the Holy Spirit. You had better take care of it! Finally, there's God's version of things or my scriptural and experiential opinion on it.

Food should be neutral. We should not be reliant on food to sustain us. Both the right and the left sides make food more powerful than Holy Spirit. My stance is we rely on Holy Spirit to sustain us. In trusting Him, food becomes neutral. We won't overeat or eat ten pounds of sugar because our focus is in the right place. Neither will we spend hours counting calories or trying to sustain our health through our diet.

This chapter is not to get you to change your diet one way or the other. It isn't giving you permission to go hog wild. Rather, it is to put diet in its proper perspective. My health isn't reliant on the food consumed. Instead, it is reliant trusting that Holy Spirit is sustaining me. Many people point to the Old Testament and claim the food restrictions are there to point the way to good health. This just isn't true. God uses the physical to show us the spiritual. He placed the dietary restrictions in place as a means to lead us into spiritual truth. He used it at first to separate the children of Israel from the gentiles. Then, it was used to show that whoever believes in Christ is His Chosen people.

A doctrine, in order to be legitimate, there should be two or more "witnesses" or scriptural references. Let me show you how Holy Spirit is not limited by our diet and our health is not determined by what we put into our mouth.

> *There is nothing from without a man, that entering into him can defile him: but the things which come out of him, those are they that defile the man. (Mark 7:15)*

> *And he saith unto them, Are ye so without understanding also? Do you not perceive, that whatsoever thing from without entereth into the man, it cannot defile him; Because it entereth not into his heart, but into the belly, and goeth out into the draught, purging all meats? (Mark 7:18-19)*

> *Therefore, I say unto you, Take no thought for your life, what ye shall eat, or what ye shall drink; nor yet for your body, what ye shall put on. Is not the life more than meat, and the body than raiment? (Matthew 6:25)*

> *Not that which goeth into the mouth defileth a man; but that which cometh out of the mouth, this defileth a man. (Matthew 15:11)*

There you go. That's only four scriptures about food which you might dismiss because you've been taught that food can affect the way the body functions. Human wisdom says what's good for you where God says a different story. You will separate the physical from the spiritual and put it off as being nonsense, that it doesn't apply to diet. Remember we talked about that? The spiritual truth applies to the physical world, there is no separation. Jesus and Paul are talking about the physical well-being of a person as much as the spiritual well-being.

> *For every creature of God is good, and nothing to be refused, if it be received with thanksgiving: For it is sanctified by the word of God and prayer. (1 Timothy 4:4-5)*

That would be five scriptures so far and counting that states all food is good for consumption. This is of course if you truly believe that and take it with prayer and thanksgiving. **Please don't be stupid.** Once again, first I must prove that Holy Spirit will keep your body healthy, separate from what you put into it. Then, I will show you why this is essential to believe this and how to make that transition without endangering yourself. Let's look at my favorite example, Peter.

For ten years after the cross, he continued to keep to the Old Covenant dietary restrictions. Not only that, but he also would separate himself from the converted gentiles whenever there were Jewish Believers around. Remember that Paul confronted Peter on this very thing three times. It took a vision from God to correct him.

> *On the morrow, as they went on their journey, and drew nigh unto the city, Peter went up upon the housetop to pray about the sixth hour: and he became very hungry, and would have eaten: but while they made ready, he fell into a trance, and saw heaven opened, and a certain vessel descending upon him, as it had been a great sheet knit at the corners, and let down to the earth: Wherein were all manner of four footed beasts of the earth, and wild beasts, and creeping things, and fowls of the air. And there came a voice to him, Rise, Peter; kill, and eat. But Peter said, Not so, Lord; for I have never eaten anything that is common or unclean. And the voice spake unto him again the second time, what God hath cleansed,*

> *that call not thou common. This was done thrice: and the vessel was received up again into heaven. (Acts 10:9-16)*

Once again, many preachers will rationalize this away, and state that is only the spiritual truth, that it really doesn't apply in the physical world. So, God purposefully used a physical thing that isn't true to show the spiritual nature. To that I need to say, "Really? so God lies?" It's a spiritual truth which makes it a physical truth. Let's look at what God spoke to Peter.

"What God hath cleansed, that call not thou common." Hello, that was God rebuking Peter over it over both how he viewed the gentiles to be unclean, and how he viewed food. Better think about it my friends! You'll still rationalize it away and say well that doesn't include the preservatives that we have today. Yes, it does. In order for it to exist, God did create what it took to manufacture the preservatives. Unless you're claiming that man can replace God and create something out of nothing. "I'm just saying." Let's look at yet another stern rebuking.

> *Now the Spirit speaketh expressly, that in the latter times some shall depart from the faith, giving heed to seducing spirits, and doctrines of devils; (1 Timothy 4:1)*
>
> *...and commanding to abstain from meats, which God hath created to be received with thanksgiving of them which believe and know the truth. (1 Timothy 4:3-4a)*

That is pretty stern calling it a doctrine of devils to teach that you should avoid foods! Yet, doctors do it, preachers do it, even the Catholics command it. That is because everything should lead to Holy Spirit in us. He is Our sustainer. You do have every right to choose what you eat. That isn't the doctrine of devils. But commanding/teaching others that they need to abstain from foods is, because that's the wisdom of men, not God. Now you are minding the things of this world. **I am not telling you to get off of**

a diet given by a doctor or that you're condemned for that diet. Don't worry! I just need to break down your rationalizing. If you have any doubts, there are still more scriptures proving we are not to rely on food, but on Holy Spirit. Do you think that I've met the required two scriptures proving the Truth or you still rationalizing? Here's another one.

> *Him that is weak in the faith receive ye, but not to doubtful disputations. For one believeth that he may eat all things: another, who is weak, eateth herbs. Let not him that eateth despise him that eateth not; and let not him which eateth not judge him that eateth: for God hath received him. (Romans 14:1-3)*

Him that is weak in faith eats herbs. That's a biggie. Let it be known, you have every right to choose what you eat. I've not got any problems with it. This isn't a matter of pride. It's a matter for you to hear the truth which will help to grow and mature you. It is taking whatever you choose to eat and relying on Holy Spirit to sustain you, not the food. It is simply meant as a change in perspective.

> *I know and am persuaded by the Lord Jesus, that there is nothing unclean of itself: but to him that esteemeth any thing to be unclean, to him it is unclean. (Romans 14:14)*
>
> *For meat destroy not the work of God. All things indeed are pure; (Romans 14:20b)*

Who's the work of God? You are. Who is the bread of Life? Jesus. Who sustains us? His Holy Spirit within us who is giving life to our mortal body. Jesus was at the well, with the Samaritan woman all day long in the hot desert sun. The disciples went into town to get some food. When they came back, they were concerned about his health. What is His answer? "I have food you don't know about," was His answer. My point is, that is proof positive, without any doubt whatsoever, that His Spirit within us will keep us healthy when we believe it. If we don't believe as the scripture above says, then to him who doesn't believe it is impure.

Now for the opposition. Do they have two scriptures to support their point of view, that I am responsible by what I eat to sustain my body? There are three scriptures they use to refute any contention that the Holy Spirit will sustain our bodies. These are:

> *I beseech you therefore, brethren, by the mercies of God, that ye present your bodies a living sacrifice holy, acceptable unto God, which is your reasonable service. (Romans 12:1)*

> *Whether therefore ye eat, or drink, or whatsoever ye do, do all to the glory of God. (1 Corinthinians 10:31)*

> *Flee fornication. Every sin that a man doeth is without the body; but he that committeth fornication sinneth against his own body. What? Know ye not that your body is the temple of the Holy Ghost which is in you, which ye have of God, and ye are not your own? (1 Corinthians 6:18-20)*

As I've already shown with an abundance of scripture, what we put into our bodies has nothing to do with being holy and acceptable to God. The last scripture in fact has nothing to do with food whatsoever, but has to do with **the only sin committed within the body, fornication.** If God is judging you by your diet, then Paul wouldn't have stated that fornication is the only sin committed within the body. Not only that, in context in verse thirteen Paul states:

> *Meats for the belly, and the belly for meats: but God shall destroy both it and them....(1 Corinthians 6:13)*

In other words, food just goes out of the body. I'm so tired of hearing your body is the temple of the Holy Spirit so you better take care of it by what you eat.

Jesus and Paul are explicitly clear that isn't the case. That statement is putting food above what Holy Spirit is capable of, telling us not to rely on Holy Spirit in us to keep us healthy, but on a physical substance. In other words, it is also like saying we can earn our salvation by our works, the ole' religious mindset. Genesis 9:3b is the kicker! *Every moving thing that liveth shall be meat for you; even as the green herb have I given you all things.*

Want more proof that relying on food doesn't keep you healthy, just go to any hospital. There are as many people who have gone to the extremes to keep themselves healthy. Yet, there they are. I knew a doctor who had a healthy diet, didn't eat pork, and exercised, who at the age of 55 years old, suddenly dropped dead. All those years he spent exercising and all the extremes he went through to keep himself healthy went out the door. It was time wasted. He was a very dear man who I loved very much. I am not mocking him at all. The things he did for our community were amazing. I admired, respected him, and miss him. In every other aspect of his life, he was a true believer.

Ok, so take a deep breath. All of that was to get you open to a change in perspective no matter your diet. The reason is so very important. Look at it this way. Even the foods that are considered healthy aren't. Your fruits, vegetables, chicken, fish all are being genetically altered. And with fruits and vegetables, there are many pesticides and poisons added. Name one food that is in a pure state unless you grow it yourself, and even then, most seeds that are bought have been genetically altered as well.

That is why it is important to get the scriptural concept that Holy Spirit is actively taking care of you. The physical senses can be difficult to overcome. It is switching from the mindset that food is sustaining you, to Holy Spirit in you is cleansing the food that will give you a long and healthy life that matters.

Having a personal relationship with Holy Spirit is what will change your focus and being aware that it is by the sacrifice of Christ's

Body that your divine health is taken care of. As you eat, do it with thanksgiving and bless your food, knowing it is Holy Spirit inside of you that is cleansing and sanctifying your food. When you bless your food, let it be more than an afterthought, believe what you are saying. Take communion which is simply remembering that Christ gave His body for yours to be healthy. It takes one second while putting the food in mouth to do it in remembrance of Him. This is switching your focus from relying on food to His Holy Spirit inside of you sustaining your body.

The same goes for medicine that you are taking. As you are taking the medicine, remember Christs sacrifice. Therefore, the medicine will do no harm. In fact, with pain medicine for instance, quit thinking that it's the pain killer removing the pain. It's Holy Spirit within you. It is a simple shift to it's all about Him. This will give you a leg up in recognizing a miracle. It's isn't the pill, it's Christ. Therefore, before you even realize it, you will need the pain pill less and less.

Overcoming all the brainwashing is a process. Don't rush it or put yourself in harm's way. All of us have been taught that food will keep us healthy, Christians more than most. Not only do you get it from doctors, but also from preachers saying it's all up to you. Listen to Holy Spirit who is inside of you. Recognizing God's truth is a start, but it's just a starting point. The common problem is we all think we're more mature than what we are. When we are relying more on Holy Spirit, then we will think less about food. We will also not binge on food. It won't be as important. We won't rely on it to be a comforter anymore. Food will become neutral. We won't overindulge.

It is just like sin. The more we focus on the Love of Christ, the less we'll sin. The more we focus on sin or not sinning, the more we will sin. Which is why food is such a huge issue, because we focus more on food than anything else, specially if we have health problems and we're told to eat properly or lose weight. So, then we struggle, struggle, and struggle.

This whole chapter isn't about eating anything you want. It's about putting food in its proper perspective. With myself having gone six months without food, I had that testimony which made my transition easy. Because there is no doubt that it was Holy Spirit in me. So, no beating yourself up. Just start accepting food with gratitude, thanksgiving, and bless the food. Remember the Lord's body as you eat, and trust Him to supernaturally provide what your body needs. The next chapter will help to clarify this even more.

17 HOLY INTIMACY

If we receive the witness of men, the witness of God is greater: for this is the witness of God which he hath testified of his Son. He that believeth on the Son of God hath the witness in himself: he that believeth not God hath made him a liar; because he believeth not the record that God gave of his Son. (1 John 5:9-10)

We hear the gospel, a person gives us a testimony of God, and we come to believe that Jesus is for real. The majority of Christians will then go to Church on Sundays, listen to a preacher and that's where it stays. A few people actually take it one more step and study scripture. All of these things are absolutely essential and needed. We stop there and that is the problem, we never get past the witness of men. Think about it. All of these things including scripture are witnesses of men. They all come from outside ourselves and into us through our physical senses. All can be manipulated by others and ourselves. We may not hear correctly. They may not be speaking correctly. We may not be reading the words correctly. All these things are subject to the things of the physical world and our physical senses. These things are all the witness of men including (gasp for air in shock) written scriptures. There is only one witness that can be one hundred percent relied upon. *He that believeth on the Son of God hath the witness in himself.* That would be the Spirit of Christ within us. The numbers of people that reach this point are few but growing. The Godhead within us is the only True teacher, comforter, and witness bearing witness to ourselves that we are in fact children of God.

The level that we walk in this life is a direct reflection of our relationship with Holy Spirit. If what is written in the pages of this book leads you into a closer relationship and a closer reliance upon Him, then the mission is accomplished. You will then walk into a fuller life, seeing and experiencing amazing things. Then, you will start walking in more love for others as never before and set more people free from the oppression of this world. Relationship is therefore crucial and you can't have a close relationship without communication. The deeper the communication, the deeper the relationship.

An example of this is a marriage. If my wife and I only use a verbal language, then there will be limits to our how close our bond is. Without a deeper knowing of each other, our relationship will only go to a minimal level. The same is true with Holy Spirit. What should be the closest relationship we've ever experienced will be extremely limited. Most Believers' experiences are limited to reciting a list of needs or maybe some written prayers. This ain't going to cut it, buttercup.

There is so much more than just a list of needs (that's already taken care of and known) or some Holy prayer that's someone's written and says is so powerful. Those formula prayers aren't an intimate deep personal relationship. What if your husband or wife gave you a pretty letter from a friend who wrote that letter to their spouse? You'd have every right to be offended. Yet, that is what we do to the Holy Person that is inside of us. We never get to know His Language or how He speaks to us. Therefore, we never get to know with deep meaning that He is in us giving life to our bodies.

What I'm talking about is speaking in a private prayer language or tongues as it's commonly called. A brave few of you attend a church that speaks in tongues, for instance a Pentecostal or Charismatic church. Yet, even then it is with other people in attendance, and you're all speaking it together. It's like having dinner with another couple. It's good to do. Everyone can enjoy themselves. But if that's the only communication you have with your wife, it's not enough. The way I've seen it done in Pentecostal churches, it's a shouting match to see who can out scream the other person, which isn't intimate at all. That would be like having dinner with a couple and the men are arguing about which football team is better. There is nothing deep about the conversation at all. The women then feel left out and nothing was attained. Oh, everyone leaves church that day feeling great. Then, reality sweeps in and Holy Spirit is in you, forgotten about till next Sunday. You never learn how to function with Holy Spirit being in an intimate partnership with Him. He is one spirit with you!

My speaking in my private prayer language was untaught of by men. Since no one taught it to me, I don't have all the nonsense teachings from it. That should be the way it is with everyone. But with all things, men get their hands involved, and it becomes full of rules and regulations that don't exist. The prayer language should naturally evolve. But we stop it and cut it short based on whose teaching we believe. We let our physical, unrenewed minds talk us out of it, thinking it's nonsense. Where our example comes from also scares a lot of people off. If I hadn't already been speaking in tongues, when I went to one Pentecostal church, I probably would never had tried. It was done with such nonsense it's unreal.

Actually, if I recall correctly, my first experience with it was before my healing, before I had actually accepted Christ. I was using the walker and this little old lady came up to me outside the church parking lot. She asked to pray for me. Unknowingly, I said ok. She put her hand on my shoulder and started speaking this gibberish. If I hadn't been holding onto the walker for dear life, I would've knocked her out. Hey! Give me a break! This was when I was still an unbeliever. Just don't do that to people. I guarantee that it did nothing to help the situation.

Here's what your personal prayer language will do. It will strengthen your inner man. It will build you up and give you a close connection with the Holy Spirit. The Holy Spirit within in you is teaching without the use of your known language. A deep connection is then formed. The more you speak it, the deeper the connection. Over time, this will cause an even deeper connection that is without words of any sort. Most of my prayer life is in tongues, but now it's even deeper than that. It is more like a tone or vibration deep inside my spirit and I just know what it means. I've been given many revelations through this way. My prayer language is very private and personal. I don't just blurt it out anytime. Yet, just like a conversation with my wife, I have access to it at any time. I stop it and start it back up. When I first started speaking in my prayer language, it was out loud. Then a few years ago, it shifted to being deeper and not so much out loud verbalizing. This was after about three years of speaking it out loud whenever I was alone. I would speak it as I was actively doing things. The more you speak it out, the more of a language it becomes, the deeper relationship you then have.

Anyone that is reading this needs to be encouraged to speak in their prayer language. You are one spirit with the Lord, so there is no waiting for it. As it is with anything else in God's Kingdom, believe that you have it, eagerly anticipate speaking it, then just open your mouth, engage your vocal cords, and whatever comes out is good. If it's a grunt, then grunt. It doesn't matter. It's just like I've described with healing. Just recognize that you're communicating with Holy Spirit inside of you. He's doing the verbalizing, but you are opening your mouth and engaging your vocal cords. This isn't a left brain or right brain thing, it is coming from deep within your spirit.

Your personality won't change. You're already one spirit with Him. It doesn't have to look freaky as it's often portrayed. It's just you communicating with another person who is an integral part of you. You will often feel energized. Healing can also occur. Just recognize and acknowledge the healing. Many things can happen. It is and can be a supernatural experience which should become a natural part of your life. Communicating this way will reap more benefits than you can ever imagine. Yet, it's still just a starting point.

Imagine this. In heaven, do you think we'll be talking in a spoken language? I'm writing this with the general idea of what people think heaven is like. Real reality is in the spiritual realm. Our spirits will all be linked together, therefore, no need for verbal language. This is just a starting point, here on our earthly existence.

As I write my books, I'm often speaking in my private prayer language. So, don't limit yourself or Holy Spirit inside of you. You'll experience a deeper bond than ever before if you don't let your physical senses hold you back.

The majority of people that I minister to don't have a private prayer language. My personal opinion is that, if you learn how to communicate with Holy Spirit on this intimate level, there would be less resistance to being able to recognize and acknowledge your healing. This form of communication has an unexplainable way of breaking through barriers that the physical brain puts in our way.

18 WRAPPING IT UP

That he would grant you, according to the riches of his glory, to be strengthened with might by his Spirit in the inner man; That Christ may dwell in your by faith; that ye, being rooted and grounded in love, May be able to comprehend with all saints what is the breadth, and length, and depth, and height; And to know the love of Christ, which passeth knowledge, that ye might be filled with all the fullness of God. (Ephesians 3:16-19)

I'm sitting here with tears in my eyes once again. Whenever I've finished a book, it always ends with happy tears. I just know that I've shared everything that I've got to share with you for this period of time. Update on hurricane Florence: They are now saying that it will hit land at a category 2 strength; That is down from a category 4 or 5 they were predicting. It is my belief that the supernatural will happen and when it touches shore, it will unexplainably go to just a tropical storm. No lives will be lost, in Jesus Name. The scripture in Ephesians is my prayer for you, that you grow and mature and truly know and experience the Love of Christ in ways you never have before.

We've only scratched the surface of what is possible with Holy Spirit inside of us, Christ is on the throne. I do believe, before long, believers will be speaking and food will supernaturally grow. Barren ground will become lush with food of all types. Starvation will be nominal, divine health will become the normal, and the need for healthcare will begin to vanish away. Scoff if you will. But Christ will return when we have learned to walk in His Stature, not before. The brighter we who are His Body shine, the closer to seeing the truth will be. So, live each day spreading His Love throughout the world. Then, the darkness will fade with the Light of Christ.

Hey! Do me a favor, right now! See Holy Spirit giving life to your body. Move around with eager anticipation that you *will* recognize improvement. That pain you experienced before is gone. The body part that wouldn't move before is moving. The kidney that was functioning less than perfectly is now in perfect condition. Thank you, Jesus! Now get out there! Live a vibrant and healthy life. Pray for others and see them healed. Be a light where it is needed the most. Will you do that for me? Please drop me an email with any testimonies that you have. I look forward to hearing from you. An Amazon Review will also be extremely helpful. Remember that you are loved by myself, and more importantly, by The Father, Jesus, and Holy Spirit.

I'm off to do some grocery shopping which I totally despise. Maybe we'll meet there and you can do my shopping for me! *Be Blessed, Be*
Healed, and Be a Blessing! Much Love, my friends.

ABOUT THE AUTHOR

Tony Myers is author of the books "The Lord Jesus Healed Me" and "Unlocking the Mystery of Diving Healing." He lives in Virginia with his precious wife Deb and all their four legged family members. A former atheist who was healed from Lou Gehrig's disease, this illness left him paralyzed and dying. Then, he was suddenly healed by Christ.

Since his healing on July 4th, 2012, he has appeared as a guest on many different platforms and media. This includes radio, television, and of course the internet. Most of his time is spent on his business and ministering the Gospel of Christ to others. The planned future holds more speaking engagements and more books to come. Tony is very open to be contacted for prayer, ministry, book signings, and for opportunities to preach the Gospel of Christ.

Check out his website tonybelieves.com,
Facebook @tonyjustbelieves or
email: tonyjustbelieves@gmail.com

MORE FROM TONY

After living a life of atheism, Tony Myers was fighting for his life. He was completely paralyzed, and his body was shutting down. Diagnosed with Lou Gehrig's disease, a debilitating neurological disease with no cure or treatment options, all hope was lost. Then suddenly one day, Tony, determined to end his own life, found a miracle healing instead!

During this journey you will cry, laugh, feel his wife's heartache, and then finally have a tremendous burst of joy as you celebrate his miracle with him and his wife Deb. Tony's honest, folksy telling of his story will make you believe he's sitting right in front of you drinking coffee! This story will encourage, motivate, and inspire you to believe in a miracle for yourself. If you are need of hope and encouragement, then this book is for you.

This book is the field manual as far as receiving healing for yourself is concerned. It is meant to awaken in the readers the mind of Christ and help them tap into the God-realm (i.e., "kingdom of heaven"). That's where we can receive the riches of Christ provided to us by grace. specifically, divine health and healing.

Before you close this book, please go to amazon and leave a review. Thank you very much!

Made in the USA
Middletown, DE
22 September 2019